Dogsong

and Related Readings

McDougal Littell
A HOUGHTON MIFFLIN COMPANY

Evanston, Illinois   *Boston*   *Dallas*

Acknowledgments

Simon & Schuster Children's Publishing Division: *Dogsong* by Gary Paulsen. Copyright © 1985 by Gary Paulsen. This edition is reprinted by arrangement with Simon & Schuster Books for Young Readers, Simon & Schuster Children's Publishing Division.

The Estate of Knud Rasmussen: "Glorious it is to see," Copper Eskimo poem from *I Breathe a New Song*, edited by Richard Lewis. Reprinted by permission of the Sand & Sørensen law firm, Copenhagen, counsel for the estate of Knud Rasmussen.
Richard Lewis: "Signal Song on Capture of Polar Bear" and "Paddler's Song on Bad Hunting Weather," Ammassalik Eskimo poems from *I Breathe a New Song*, edited by Richard Lewis. Copyright © 1971 by Richard Lewis. Published by Simon and Schuster. Reprinted by permission of Richard Lewis.
Little, Brown and Company: Excerpt from "Susan Butcher," from *Champions* by Bill Littlefield. Text Copyright © 1993 by Bill Littlefield. Illustrations Copyright © 1993 by Bernie Fuchs. By permission of Little, Brown and Company.
Keith Ross Leckie: *Words on a Page* by Keith Ross Leckie. Reprinted by permission of the author.

Continued on page 208

The editors have made every effort to trace the ownership of all copyrighted selections found in this book and to make full acknowledgment for their use. Omissions brought to our attention will be corrected in a subsequent edition.

Cover illustration by Lee Christiansen.

ISBN-13: 978-0-395-77527-1   ISBN-10: 0-395-77527-2

11 12 13 14 15 16 17 18 - DCI - 09 08 07 06

Contents

Dogsong

Gary Paulsen

Part One

···

The Trance

Chapter 1

I *came wet into the world.*
On both sides there were cliffs,
white cliffs that were my mother's thighs.
And I didn't cry though it was cold
by the white cliffs and I was afraid.
I came wet into the world.

—an old Eskimo man relating
the memory of his birth in a
snowhouse on the sea ice.

Russel Susskit rolled out of the bunk and put his feet on the floor and listened in the darkness to the sounds of morning.

They were the same sounds he had always heard, sounds he used to listen for. Now in the small government house—sixteen by twenty—they grated like the ends of a broken bone.

He heard his father get up and hack and cough and spit into the stove. His father smoked cigarettes all day, rolled them with Prince Albert tobacco, and had one hanging on his lip late into the night. In the mornings he had to cough the cigarettes up. The sound tore at Russel more than at his father. It meant something that did not belong on the coast of the sea in a small Eskimo village. The coughing came from Outside, came from the tobacco which came from

Outside and Russel hated it.

After the coughing and spitting there was the sound of the fire being lit, a sound he used to look forward to as he woke. The rustle of paper and kindling and diesel fuel, which was used to start the wood, the scratch of a match, the flame taking and the stink of the diesel oil filling the one room. Russel did not like the smell of the diesel oil but he did not hate it the way he hated his father's coughing in the morning.

Russell heard the wind outside and that was good except that it carried the sounds of the village waking, which meant the sound of snowmachine engines starting up.

The snowmachines were loud and scared the seals. To fourteen-year-old Russel the whine of them above the wind hurt as much as the sound of coughing. He was coming to hate them, too.

It was still dark in the house because the village generator hadn't been turned on for the day. The darkness was cut by the light of the oil lamp on the table as his father touched a match to the wick.

Flat light filled the room and Russel looked around as he always did. It was a standard government house—a winter house. They would move to summer fish-camps later. But in the winter they came into the village and stayed in the government houses. Boxes is what they are, really, he thought: boxes to put people in.

In one corner there was a small table with an oilcloth table cover. The cloth was patterned with roses and Russel did not know why his father had ordered it. There were no women there. Russel's mother had been gone for years, gone with a white trapper. But his father had liked the roses on the tablecloth and had sent for it. Russel had never seen

"Dogs are like ite people," Oogruk said, looking at the flame hey do not know how to get a settled mind. They always turning, looking for a better way to lie do . And if things go wrong they have anger and frust on. They are not like us. It is said that dogs and w people come from the same place." He snorted— nasal sound, a kind of *chaa* sound through his se that could have meant anything from scorn anger to humor. "I do not know how true tha because white people are clearly not dogs. Bu hey have many of the same ways and so one wo rs."

Russel nodded but id nothing. One time he had seen a bushpilot who d crashed his plane near the village. The plane wa roken in the middle and the pilot had stood scre ing at it and kicking it for failing him and fallin rom the sky. He treated the plane like a living an il until he got tired, then he walked away as a dog ould walk away from a stick he'd been tearing at.

Oogruk sighed. "I ll tell you about something. We used to have son for everything, and nobody knows the songs an ore. There were songs for dogs, for good dogs o ad dogs, and songs to make them work or track be . There were songs for all of everything. I used to k ow a song that would make the deer come to me that I could kill it. And I knew a man who cou sing a song for whales and make them come to hi harpoon."

The flame guttered n the lamp and Russel saw Oogruk use a small iv ry tool to brush the burned moss away to clean t flame. A new-yellow filled the room, cut through he smoke, then paled down as the twisted moss bu ed on the end.

Russel shifted and uck his legs out straight in front of him—Eskim fashion—and relaxed. He leaned back against the wall. There were things he wanted to ask but he did not know what they were. Part of his mind was turning over, but another part was full of a strange patience and so he waited. Sometimes it was better to wait.

"Mebbe you could bring in those eyes and put some snow in the pot and we'll warm them up. Cold eyes are bad to eat."

Russel got up and went outside. The wind was stronger now, bringing cold off the ice, but he didn't wear a coat and liked the tightness the cold caused when it worked inside his light shirt. He used his belt knife to pop the caribou eyes out of the two skulls—they levered out with surprising difficulty—and stopped by the door to take down the pan hanging on the wall and fill it with snow.

He put the eyes on top and took the pan and snow inside and handed them to Oogruk, who held the pan over the lamp.

"One misses women," the old man said. "I had some good wives but they are gone. Two died back before the white men came, died bearing children, and the last one just left. She went up to the mining town to a party and didn't come back. One misses women."

Russel said nothing. He was seated again, leaning against the wall, and as with dogs he knew nothing of women. The girls smiled at him with round faces and merry eyes but he was not ready for women yet and so knew nothing of them.

"They cooked and sewed for me. Eyes and meat taste better when cooked by women. That's the truth."

Russel had never eaten eyes. He knew the fluid in them would be too salty. He smiled. "Were there songs for the women, too?" He wanted Oogruk to talk of the songs again.

Tonight in the village he would let it be known that he was a new person, not the old Russel, and he would tell the story to Oogruk and anybody who would listen, the story of how he took the deer with the arrow that flew across the dark.

And the telling would become part of the song.

Chapter 4

Those white men came a long time ago. The white men who talked with rocks in their mouths. They came and took and took it all. They used our men as beasts and they took our women for their own and left us with no meat. Left us starving. They took all the fur and then they left. That is what I was told when I was young and in those villages they still don't like the white men who talk with rocks in their mouth.

—Eskimo speaking about the
early Russian fur hunters
who came for pelts.

Sea ice is not the same as fresh-water ice. The salt-water ice is stronger, more elastic, isn't as slippery. Also the sea ice moves all the time, even when it is thick. Sometimes whole cakes of the ice will go out to sea, miles across, sliding out to sea and taking anybody on the cake with it.

On the fourth day after taking the deer with the arrow Russel took the team out on the ice to find seals. Oogruk wanted oil for the lamp and he wanted some seal meat and fat to eat and he said these things in such a way that Russel felt it would be good to find a seal to take with the harpoon. It wasn't that he actually asked, or told Russel to go for seal, but he talked about how it was to hunt in the old days.

"Out on the edge of the ice, where it meets the sea but well back from the edge, sometimes there are seal holes. The seals come up through them and sit on the ice and if you are there when they come you can get the small harpoon point in them. That is the way it was done. Men would leave their dogs well back and pile a mound of snow in front of them and wait for the seal. Wait and wait." Oogruk had scratched with his nails on the wall of the house. "When the seal starts to come there is a scratching sound and the hunter must be ready to put the point in then."

"How long must one wait?" Russel asked.

"There is not a time. Waiting for seals is not something you measure. You get a seal, that is all. Some men go a whole winter and get none, some will get one right away. Hunting seals with the small point and the killing lance is part of the way to live."

So Russel went out on the ice. He took the team away in the daylight and was twenty miles out, working heavily through pressure ridges, when the storm came off the sea.

He had seen many storms. In his years with the village, every winter brought violent storms off the sea, white walls of wind and driven snow. Twice he had been caught out on a snowmachine and had to run for the village ahead of the wall coming across the ice.

But with a dog team you did not run ahead of the wall. As he was crossing a pressure ridge, pushing the dogs up and over the broken, jagged edges, he heaved up on the sled and looked out across the ice, out to sea, and a great boiling wall of white was rising to the sky. In seconds it was impossible to tell where the sky ended and the sea ice began and Russel knew he would have to hide before it hit. He fought the sled down the pressure ridge and brought the dogs around into a small hole under an overlapping ice ledge. There was barely room to pull his legs in.

He tipped the sled over to make a rough door across the opening to block the wind and pulled the dogs in on top of him. Working as fast as he could he tried to pack snow into the slats of the sled bottom but before he could make any headway the wind roared into the pressure ridge.

Russel drew the hood tight on his parka and huddled into the dogs, closing the small opening in the front of his hood by burying his face in dog fur.

The dogs whined for a few moments, then squirmed into better positions, with their noses under their tails, and settled in to ride the storm out the same way dogs and wolves have ridden storms out forever—by sleeping and waiting.

Russel felt a couple of small wind-leaks around the edge of his parka and he stopped them by pulling the drawstrings tighter at the parka's bottom hem. When he had all air movement stopped he could feel the temperature coming up in his clothing and he listened to the wind as it tore at his shelter.

In what seemed like moments but might have been an hour, the wind had piled a drift over his hole and he used a free arm to pack the snow away and clear the space around his body. The dogs remained still and quiet, their heat tight around Russel.

After a time he dozed, and when he awakened it seemed that the wind had diminished to some degree. He used a mittened hand to clear away a hole and he saw that it was getting darker—the short day almost gone again—and that indeed the wind was dying.

He stood, broke through the drift and shrugged the snow off. It was still cloudy but everything seemed to be lifting. The dogs were curled in small balls covered with snow, each of them completely covered except for a small blowhole where a breath had kept the snow melted. Each hole had a tiny bit of steam puffing up as the dogs exhaled and Russel was reluctant to make them stir. They looked so comfortable in their small houses.

Still he had to get home.

"Ha! Hay! Everybody up!" He grabbed the gangline and shook it. The leader stood up and shook his fur clean of snow and that brought the rest of them up. Slowly they stretched and three of them evacuated, showing they understood work. A good dog will always leave waste before going to work, to not carry extra on the run.

In a minute he had them lined out, aimed for home—or where he thought the village was—and when he called them to run they went about thirty yards and stopped. It wasn't abrupt. They were running and they slowed to a trot and then a walk and finally they just stopped.

"What is it?" Russel snorted. "Are we still asleep in our houses? Hai! Get it up and go."

Again they started and went forty or so yards and stopped.

Russel swore. "Get up! Run now or I will find a whip."

And after a time, hesitating still, they finally got moving. Slowly. At a trot first, then a fast walk, then back up to a trot, they headed across the ice fields.

Russel nodded in satisfaction. He had not run dogs enough to know for certain what it meant when they didn't want to run, but he supposed that it was because they had anticipated staying down for a longer time.

But the man had to run the dogs. That's what Oogruk had said to him. "You must be part of the dogs, but you must run them. If you do not tell them what to do and where to go they will go where they want. And where a dog wants to go is not always the same as where the man wants to go."

The wind had stopped almost as suddenly as it came, in the way of arctic storms, but before it died it seemed to have changed a bit. When it first came it was out of the west, straight in from the sea, but before it stopped Russel noted that it had moved around to the north, was coming down from the blue-black north, the cold places.

Twice more the dogs tried to come to the right, but he made them go back and run his way. At last they lined out and went to work and Russel looked for the lights of the village. He had come out a way, but as the wind died he knew they should show, especially the light up on the hill near the fuel tanks.

He saw nothing. The clouds were still thick and low so he couldn't see the stars. He had nothing to help him tell his true direction.

He ran for several hours, letting the dogs seek their own speed, and once he was sure he should have run into the village he called them down and set the snowhook.

He was going the wrong way.

What has happened, he thought, is that during the storm the ice has caked and turned. A whole, huge plate of ice with Russel and the dogs had rotated and changed all his directions. That's why the dogs had hesitated, held back. They knew the way home and had wanted to head back to the house.

He could have let them run and they would have taken him home. But now—now what would they do?

More now, he thought. More is coming now. It was getting cold, colder than he'd ever seen it. He could feel the cold working into his clothing, see the white steam of the dog's breath coming back over their backs. His feet were starting to hurt. He was lost and the cold was working in and he did not know where to go.

There were just the dogs—the dogs and the sled and him. And the ice, and the snow and the northern night. Nobody would come to look for him because they expected him to be out late—or didn't expect anything at all. He had told nobody other than Oogruk that he was going out for seals and since he was staying at Oogruk's house nobody else could know that he was gone. And Oogruk would not expect him back because Russel was hunting the old way.

He was alone.

And a part of him grew afraid. He had seen bad weather many times. But he'd always had the chance to get out of it. On a snowmachine, unless it broke down, you could ride to safety. But he would have to face the cold now.

He debated what to do for three or four minutes. If he went down without a fire the cold would get bad later—maybe too bad. He had nothing to burn and there was no wood or fuel on the ice.

And what had Oogruk said about that? He fought to remember the trance but nothing came. He knew about problems growing in the cold, or during a storm, from other people. But Oogruk had said nothing about being lost on the ice.

Lost on the ice.

People died when they were lost on the ice. He had heard stories of people dying, of whole families lost. The ice moved out and away from land and the people had starved to death or drowned when the ice broke up beneath them, stories that came down in the long nights, sad stories.

And now Russel. Now Russel lost on the ice with a dog team and sled.

In the sled bag he had a small piece of meat left over from when he and Oogruk had cooked the deer. He could eat. That would help him stay warm. And then what?

He could wait until the clouds cleared off and he could see stars and they would guide him home. But it might be many days. Sometimes the clouds stayed for weeks.

"So." He talked aloud to the dogs, saw a couple of tails wag in the darkness with his voice. "So there is some trouble. What should we do?"

The leader looked around at him, although it was too dark for Russel to see his face. Still, there was something there, a desire to understand or to help. Russel smiled, a quick sign back in the fur of his hood.

The dogs.

They were the answer. He could not trust himself, couldn't see anything to help him, but he could trust the dogs. Or he thought he could. He would let them run and decide where to go.

"Hai! Enough rest. It is time to take me home. Take me back to the village."

He squeaked with his lips and they got up and started off. At first they traveled in the direction Russel had forced them to go. But as they settled into their trot the leader moved them gently to the right, more and more to the right until he had them going where he had first started them off before Russel had corrected him.

Russel nodded, let them run. They had a purpose in their backs, a pulling sense that he could believe in. He was learning about dogs, just in the few runs he'd taken. He was learning.

And one thing he had to know was that in some ways they were smarter than men. Oorgruk had said that to him.

"Men and dogs are not alike, although some men try to make them so. White men." Oogruk had laughed. "Because they try to make people out of dogs and in this way they make the dogs dumb. But to say that a dog is not smart because it is not as smart as a man is to say that snow is not smart. Dogs are not men. And as dogs, if they are allowed to be dogs, they are often smarter than men."

The problem, Russel knew, was learning when to recognize that dogs were smart. The dogs knew how to run in the dark and see with their heads, with their feet, with their hair and noses. They saw with everything.

At last Russel *knew* that they were heading back for the village in the cold and dark, knew it because he felt it inside.

But they were not home yet.

Running in the dark, even in the tight dark of the north when there is no moon, it is possible to see out ahead a great distance. The snow-ice is white-blue in the dark and if there is no wind to blow the snow around, everything shows up against the white.

Now, suddenly, there was a dark line ahead of the lead dog. A dark line followed by a black space on the snow, an opening of the ice. A lead of open water, so wide Russel could not see across.

Open water. Steam rising into the cold. The ice was moving and he was moving with it.

The team stopped. The lead dog whined and moved back and forth across the edge of the ice. The dogs hated open water, hated to get wet, but they knew that the way home was across the lead.

For a few moments the leader continued to whine

and pull back and forth. "Haw! We go left along the ice and see."

The leader slammed to the left gratefully, happy to be relieved of the responsibility.

But the open lead was long. They ran mile after mile along the broken edge of the ice, in and out of the steam wraiths that came from the sea water. New ice was forming rapidly in the deep cold but it was not safe and would not be safe for several days, if then. Besides, it kept breaking away with the shifting of the cake that Russel was running on.

Yet the fear was gone. The fear had come from the unknown, from not acting, and now that he had made a decision to act the fear had gone. He might not make it, he might die on the ice, but he would not die with fear. He would die working to not die.

That was something he could tell Oogruk when he got back. If he got back. The thing with dying was to try to not die and make death take you with surprise.

And with the end of the fear came a feeling of strength. The cold was less strong along the lead because the warmth from the sea water came up as steam. The steam froze on everything, on the gangline and the sled and the dogs. Soon everything glistened with ice, even the dogs looked like jewels running ahead of him in the dark with the ice frozen on their backs.

It was a beauty he could not measure. As so much of running the dogs proved to be—so much of it had a beauty he saw and took into himself but could not explain.

And while he was looking at the beauty he saw that the lead had narrowed. There was still open water, but there were large chunks floating in it and the idea came to him of bridging the open water with one of the chunks.

He stopped the team.

The leader whined. It is perhaps possible that Oogruk has done this, Russel thought, and the dog is scared because he's done it before.

Or it was possible that the dog was reading Russel's mind and knew what they were going to do. Or it might be that the dog had figured out what had to be done on his own.

Whatever the reason, the dog knew and he didn't like it. Russel set the hook and took the harpoon with the line on it out of the sled. He walked to the edge of the lead, holding back to make sure he wouldn't break off the edge and fall in. Death would come instantly with the water. With the weight of the parka and pants wet, he would go down like a stone.

There were several chunks floating in the lead, which had now narrowed to thirty or so feet. Most of them were smaller than he could use, but one was about twenty feet long and four feet wide. It lay sideways, halfway across the opening.

He lay the harpoon line on the ice, in a small loop, and held one end with his left hand. With his right he hefted the harpoon and with an easy toss threw it across the large chunk of ice.

Then he tried to ease it back so that the butt end of the harpoon would hang up on an edge. It was harder than it looked and took him ten or twelve tries before the harpoon shaft caught in a small hole. When it drew tight the point jammed and he took up the strain until he had the weight of the chunk moving. Slowly he pulled the ice through the dark water, slowly and gently heaving on the great weight.

He gradually brought the chunk across the lead until the end butted against the edge he stood on, then, using the harpoon as a prod he jammed and pushed until the ice lay the long way across the lead.

When it was in position he went back to the sled and pulled out the hook. "Up! Up and across the ice."

The leader knew what he wanted, but he held back, whining louder now. The ice didn't look that steady, didn't look safe. He didn't move to the side, but he wouldn't go, either.

Twice more Russel urged him from the sled but the dog wouldn't go and Russel threw the sled over on its side and walked to the front. The leader shook and crouched down but didn't move away. Russel took his mittens off and hung them by their cords behind his back. Then he grabbed a handful of hair on the dog's neck and another at the root of his tail and heaved the dog out onto the chunk.

The leader fought for balance, found it on the teetering ice, then drove with all his might for the other side of the lead, clawing and scrabbling.

So powerful was his tearing struggle that he pulled the next two dogs after him, and those three then pulled the rest of the team and the sled in a great leap onto the floating ice bridge.

Russel grabbed the handle as it went by and barely got his feet on the runners. A kick left, another to the right and the sled flew across the gap of water at the far end, splashed once as Russel threw his feet up to stay out of the water—and he was across.

Across onto the land ice. Off the floating pack ice. Safe.

Safe with the dogs. Safe and heading for the village. Safe and moving to where he could now see the light of the fuel tank on the hill. Safe out of the steam of the water and back on the solid ice.

Chapter 5

Shamans had great power in the old times before the church came. They could make stones talk, and the snow, and I knew one once that had two heads that talked to each other. They fought all the time, those two heads, and finally it was said that one of the heads told the body to kill the other. This it did and of course that made the whole body die. Shamans had great power but they weren't always smart.

—an old woman's memory.

Russel had moved away from life in the village but he was not rebelling. He was working toward something in his mind, not away from something he didn't like. He had moved in with Oogruk, but his father knew it and approved.

There was school, of course. He was not going to school but he was learning and everybody knew that; it would have been hard to stop him trying to learn what he wanted and needed to know and so nobody tried. It would not have been polite to try it and many considered Russel old enough to know what he was doing.

Life in the village went on as it had before. Men took snowmachines out on the ice to find seals, when they could get through the leads. Other hunters took other snowmachines back into the hills and found caribou, sometimes killing six or seven to bring back for other people who could not hunt.

In the long darkness house life took on a meaning that couldn't exist in the summer. Families sometimes moved in with each other for a time, played games, fought the boredom that could come with the semi-arctic night. The village had a game room with television and it was usually crowded with both adults and children, watching the outside world.

All but Russel.

And Oogruk.

Russel hunted caribou twice more but didn't get any meat either time. He saw them at a distance, but couldn't get the sled close enough to make a stalk and a kill. On the second attempt he set the hook, left the dogs, and with the bow worked up some small creek beds but the deer saw him before he could get close enough for a shot. He took rabbits and ptarmigan home each time, using a small net Oogruk had fashioned and showed him how to use. With the net, laying it on the ground and using a long line, he lured the birds with a handful of berries. When they were on the net he flicked it closed with a jerk of his wrist and caught five and six birds at a time.

So he made meat. Light meat. That's what Oogruk called it. And it was good meat, as far as it went. The small birds tasted sweet and were tender and soft, which suited Oogruk's poor teeth.

But the dogs needed heavy meat, heavy red meat and fat or they could not work, could not run long and hard.

And heavy meat meant deer. Caribou.

Or seal.

So it came on a cold clear morning that Russel

decided to go out for seal again. It was still dark when he awakened and sat up on the floor but before he could get his pants on Oogruk was sitting up and had lighted the lamp.

"It is time for me to go out for seals again. For food for the dogs. I will go out on the ice."

Oogruk nodded. "Yes. Yes. I know that. But this time I will go with you."

Russel stopped, his bearskin pants halfway up. He looked at the old man. "To hunt seals?"

"That. And other things. There are certain things that must be done at this time and it is for an old man to do them when the time is right."

Russel waited but Oogruk said nothing further. Instead he stood, slightly stiff, and feeling with his hands found clothes on the side wall. He dressed in pants and mukluks and another squirrelskin underparka. Then he took down an older outerparka, of deerskin, one with holes and worn places, and shrugged it on over his head.

"I have the good parka," Russel said. "Let me give it to you."

Oogruk shook his head. "Not this time. You keep it. You will need it and I won't. Go now and harness the dogs."

Russel finished dressing and went out for the team. They knew him now, knew him well, and greeted him with tails and barks when they saw him take the harness off the pegs. He laid the gangline out onto the snow and harnessed the team quickly, wondering why the old man wanted to go.

When the dogs were harnessed he took the weapons—two harpoons and one killing lance with a plain sharpened point—and tied them into the sled. When he turned back to the house Oogruk had come out of the door and was looking across the ice.

His milk-white eyes stared across the ice. But he was seeing nothing. Or, Russel thought, maybe he was seeing everything.

"I smell the sea out there," Oogruk said. "It is not too far today. The ice lets the smell come across."

"The dogs are harnessed."

"I know."

"Would you drive them?"

"No. I will ride. Put me in the sled and you drive."

Russel took his hand and put him in the sled, settling him back against the crosspieces at the back. When Oogruk was settled Russel pulled the hook and called the dogs up.

They tore away from the buildings and out across the ice. When he was away on the ice and the fire was burned out of them a bit he dragged the brake down and slowed them and looked back at the village.

Small gray buildings and caches on the dirty snow of the beach, with people here and there. Someone he did not recognize waved at him and he waved back. Dirty smoke came from chimneys and slid off with the wind and he watched as they moved away, picked up speed on the clean ice-snow, until he rounded the point heading north and the buildings were gone.

He waited for some kind of sadness to come but it did not, did not, and he turned back to the sled and the dogs lined out in front and he moved them over to the right a little, using a soft "Gee," to let them know it was a gentle turn. The sea was a blue line on the horizon when they crossed the high points and could see ahead.

Oogruk said nothing, but when they got within a couple of miles of the sea and the spray smell was heavy in the cold air he held up his mittened hand to signal a halt.

"There will be seals. Watch for seals." His voice

was excited, hushed but alive. "They will be on the edge of the ice. Watch for them."

Russel looked out on the edge of the ice but saw no seals. The light was half gone now and he knew that he would have to leave the sled to hunt.

"I will leave you with the dogs and go out on foot."

But now Oogruk shook his head. "No. No. It is time to talk one more time and I must leave you. But I wanted to come out here for it because I missed the smell of the sea. I wanted to smell the sea one more time."

Russel looked down in the sled at the old man. "You're leaving me?"

"Yes. But first I must tell you what to do . . ."

"Where are you going?"

"It is time to leave," Oogruk said simply. "It is my time. But there is a thing you must do now to become a man. You must not go home."

"Not go home? I do not understand."

"You must leave with the dogs. Run long and find yourself. When you leave me you must head north and take meat and see the country. When you do that you will become a man. Run as long as you can. That's what used to be. Once I ran for a year to find good birds' eggs. Run with the dogs and become what the dogs will help you become. Do you understand?"

Russel remembered now when Oogruk had said he would take a long journey. He spoke quietly. "I think so. But you, what are you to do?"

"You will leave me here on the ice, out here by the edge of the sea."

"With respect, Grandfather, I can't do that. There is a doctor. Things can be done if something is bothering you."

Oogruk shook his head. "An old man knows when death is coming and he should be left to his own on it. You will leave me here on the ice."

"But . . ."

"You will leave me here on the ice."

Russel said nothing. He didn't help Oogruk, but the old man got out of the sled himself. When he was standing on the ice he motioned Russel away. "Go now."

Russel couldn't. He held back, held the sled. "I will stay with you."

"You will go." The milk-eyes looked through him to the sea, to the snow, to the line of blue that was the sky. "You will go now."

And there was such strength in his voice that Russel knew he must go. He took the handlebar in one hand and pulled the hook, and the dogs surged away and Russel let them run without looking back. He went mile after mile, and finally he could stand it no more and he called the team around and headed back, his eyes scanning the ice in sweeps as they ran.

When they were still half a mile from where Oogruk had gotten off, Russel could see his small figure sitting on the ice and he smiled.

He would talk the old man into riding back to the village, that's all there was to it. The old man would come back and tell him more about living the old way, would sit at night and tell the stories that made the winter nights short.

But when he drew close he saw that Oogruk was sitting still. Very still. His hands were folded in his lap and his legs were stretched out in front of him and the eyes were open and not blinking with life.

Russel stopped the team before the dogs were close to Oogruk and walked ahead on foot.

Oogruk did not turn his head but stared out to

sea, out past the edge of ice where his spirit had flown, out and out. His face was already freezing and there was some blown snow in the corner of his eyes that didn't melt. Russel brushed the snow away with his mitten, a small gesture he made unknowingly, and a place in him wanted to smile and another place wanted to cry. "You left too soon, Grandfather. I was coming back for you."

He stood for a time looking down at the dead old man. Then he thought of something and he went back to the sled and took the small harpoon with the ivory toggle point from the weapons lashing. He put the harpoon across Oogruk's lap so that it balanced on his knees.

"You will want to hunt seals. Use it well and make much sweet meat."

Then he went to the sled. The dogs were nervous. They smelled the death and didn't like it. The leader whined and fidgeted and was glad when Russel called them around and headed north.

Before he let them run he turned back to Oogruk one more time. "I will remember you," he said, then let the dogs go.

He would run north for a time, then cut across the ice and head northeast into the land. He had weapons and dogs and a good sled. The rest would come from the land.

Everything would come from the land.

Part Two

The Dreamrun

Chapter 6

The Run

Out.

Into the sweeps, into the great places where the land runs to the sky and into the sky until there is no land and there is no sky.

Out.

Into the distance where all lines end and all lines begin. Into the white line of the ice-blink where the mother of wind lives to send down the white death of the northern storms.

Out.

Into the mother of wind and the father of blue ice.

Russel went out where there is nothing, into the wide center of everything there is.

Into the north.

His village lay on the northern edge of the tree line. Here and there in small valleys nearby there were scrub spruce, ugly dwarfed things torn and ripped by the fierce wind. But as the run went north even these trees vanished to be replaced by small brush and gnarled grass. Snow was scarce, blown, and the landscape looked like something from another planet.

Still there is beauty, Russel thought.

It was hard to believe the beauty of that torn and forlorn place. The small mountains—large hills, really—were sculpted by the wind in shapes of rounded softness, and the light . . .

The light was a soft blue-purple during the day, a gentle color that goes into the eyes and becomes part of the mind and goes still deeper and deeper to enter the soul. Soul color is the daylight.

At night, Russel knew, often the wind would die and go back to its mother and the cold would come down from the father of ice and the northern lights would come to dance.

They went from red to green and back again, moving across the sky in great pulses of joy, rippling the heavens, pushing the stars back, and were so grand to see that many people believed that they were the souls of dead-born children dancing in heaven and playing with balls of grass and leather.

Even in the wind there was beauty to Russel. The wind came from the north in a steady push that made the dogs work evenly, and the wind made the snow move, change into shapes that blended into the light of day and the soft glow from the sky at night.

Out.

When he'd gone far enough north along the coast to miss the village, Russel headed back into shore and moved up onto the land in a small gully, headed mostly north but slightly east.

He moved into the dark. He ran the dogs out and down. Ran them steadily for a full day, eighteen hours, letting them find the way. He stood on the sled's runners and moved to get away from what he knew, ran to get away from death sitting on the ice in Oogruk's form.

When the first dog started to weave with exhaustion, still pulling, but slipping back and forth as it pulled, he sensed their tiredness in the black night and stopped the team. He had a piece of meat in the sled, deer meat from a leg and he cut it in six pieces. When he'd pulled them under an overhanging ledge out of the wind and tipped the sled on its side, he fed them. But they were too tired to eat and slept with the meat between their legs.

He didn't know that they could become that tired and the knowledge frightened him. He was north, in the open, and the dogs wouldn't eat and they were over a hundred and fifty miles to anything. Without the dogs he would die.

Without the dogs he was nothing.

He'd never felt so alone and for a time fear roared in him. The darkness became an enemy, the cold a killer, the night a ghost from the underworld that would take him down where demons would tear strips off him.

He tried a bite of the meat but he wasn't hungry. Not from tiredness. At least he didn't think so.

But he knew he wasn't thinking too well, and so he lay down between the two wheel-dogs and pulled them close on either side and took a kind of sleep.

Brain-rest more than sleep. He closed his eyes and something inside him rested. The darkness came harder and the northern lights danced and he rested. He was not sure how long it might have been, but it was still dark when one of the dogs got up and moved in a circle to find a better resting position.

The dog awakened the remainder of the team and they all ate their meat with quiet growls of satisfaction that came from their stomachs up through their throats. Small rumbles that could be felt more than heard.

When they'd eaten they lay down again, not even pausing to relieve themselves. And Russel let them stay down for all of that long night. He dozed now with his eyes open, still between the two wheel-dogs, until the light came briefly.

Then he stood and stretched, feeling the stiffness. The dogs didn't get up and he had to go up the line and lift them. They shook hard to loosen their muscles and drop the tightness of sleeping long.

"Up now! Up and out."

Out.

They started north again, into a land that Russel did not know. At first the dogs ran poorly, raggedly, hating it. But inside half a mile they had settled into their stride and were a working team once more.

But they had lost weight.

In the long run they had lost much weight and it was necessary for Russel to make meat. He didn't know how long they could go without meat but he didn't think it could be long.

He had to hunt.

If he did not get meat the dogs would go down— and he was nothing without the dogs. He had to get food for them.

The light ended the dark-fears but did not bring much warmth. Only the top edge of the sun slipped into view above the horizon, so there was no heat from it.

To get his body warm again after the long night of being still he held onto the sled and ran between the runners. He would run until his breath grew short, then jump on and catch his wind, then run again. It took a few miles of that to get him warm and as soon as he was, the great hole of hunger opened in his stomach and he nearly fell off the sled.

The hunger lasted until he remembered the small

piece of meat he hadn't eaten the night before. He found it in the inside pouch of his parka and ate it. His body heat had thawed the meat and made it soft enough to chew. It was bad meat, tough meat, but it tasted so good that it made his jaws ache.

And with the meat came energy. It rippled through him, up from his stomach like something alive, something hot.

The meat brought strength into his legs and arms and made his eyes sharp. He scanned the hills ahead, the low round hills with grassy sides and small gullies between. That would be where he'd find game. The birds would be on the hillside where there was no snow to eat, but close to the snow so they could fly to the white for protection. The rabbits would be high so they could see when the wolves came. There would be mice in the grass if nothing else. All food.

He headed for the hills and reached into the sled for the bow. When he had it out he stopped the dogs and strung it, marveling again at its beauty, the laminated strips of horn and bone and wood shining in the light.

He took the quiver up and strapped it over his shoulder, letting the dogs run again as he worked. He would hunt with the team, rather than stalk, and hope to get close enough to something for a shot.

And now there was luck.

In many of the hills there were smaller animals. Rabbits and ptarmigan, some small fox—which had a sweet-rich meat and were easy to kill—and the ever-present mice, or lemmings. But sometimes herds of caribou numbering several hundred head moved across the land, taking the grass where they could find it.

Such a herd lay in the gully in front of Russel and the dogs. The only way out for the caribou was to run over the team, or around it. The gully had steep sides with large drifts and the deer had foolishly cornered themselves. A pack of wolves could get into them and take many of them down before they could escape. Or a man could take them. But the deer would think only of running, not where they could run, just that they could run, in blind lines.

The dogs smelled them before Russel saw them. They had seen him take the bow out and they knew he was ready to kill and when they smelled the deer they turned off and headed for the gully where the herd grazed.

There were about a hundred and fifty deer within the confines of the drifts and when the animals at the outside edge saw the dogs coming they wheeled and tried to beat Russel to the opening.

But the dogs were strong and thin and fast and they caught the deer easily. When they ran toward him into the narrowest part, Russel jumped off the sled and got ready. The dogs kept going, crazy now for the smell of deer and the wild running of the herd as it came at them.

The caribou parted around the sled and the dogs wheeled to catch them, missing most, hitting a few with the ancient hamstring tear that ripped and crippled the deer's back leg, and four of these, staggering with bloodied back legs, came by Russel.

Falling, running, they tried to keep up to the other deer but they were doomed now, as doomed as if they had been hit by wolves, and the dogs were working to catch them and pull them down.

Russel took them with arrows, putting a shaft in each one, just in back of the shoulders. He watched the arrows streak into the light and enter the deer cleanly. First one, then the other, then the next two, and they ran-fell for another fifty yards before they went down, blood spraying from their mouths onto the grass and snow.

"My arrows are true," he said aloud. And then, in a poem-song:

> *They brought the deer down,*
> *They helped the dogs to bring us meat.*
> *My arrows are true.*

The dogs were on the deer now, stopping with the first one. Russel ran over to it to hasten the death by cutting its throat but he didn't have to. The eyes were already glazing with the end and he put grass in the deer's mouth, doing the same for the second, third and fourth ones, which were already dead.

Then he pulled the dogs off and tied them away from the four carcasses. There would be food for them, but all in good time.

He would set up camp and he would skin the deer out and cut the meat for easy carrying. Then he would eat and eat, he thought, and after he ate he would sleep, and then eat more. He'd never been so hungry and he could see that the dogs were the same. They were on the edge of eating each other, fresh with the blood smell and tough with the running.

He set up camp and skinned the deer. By now it was getting dark and he cut front shoulder meat for the dogs—a great piece for each—and took a fatty tenderloin from one deer for himself. He used some grass and dried sticks and a match from his sled bag to start a fire and he warmed the meat over the flames until it was pleasant—not hot, just heated. Then he took a chunk in his mouth and bit down and cut it off by his lips with the *ulu*, wolfed it down, then another, and another, until his stomach hurt with the meat.

He mourned not having a pot, but ate snow for water and this, with the blood in the warm meat, was enough moisture to help in digestion.

With his stomach full he put one deerskin on the ground, hair side down, and the other three on top with the raw side's touching. In between the layers he had a fur sleeping bag as warm as the warmest down and he crawled in as the short-lived sun bobbed back down for the long night.

Full-bellied dogs curled into balls in their harness, sleeping next to him. Russel pulled his head under the skins, took his parka and pants off and put them outside, inside out. The moisture from his perspiration would freeze during the sleep and he would scrape the ice off in the morning. With only his squirrel parka on he pulled back into the skins, took his mukluks off and left them inside the sleeping bag to warm up and dry out.

It was a home.

The sled, the dogs, the food, and more food to eat when he awakened.

It was a home.

It was as much of a home as his people had had for thousands of years and he was content. He closed his eyes and heard the wind gently sighing outside past the hides that kept him warm and snug.

It was a home and he let his mind circle and go down, the same way a dog will circle before taking the right bed.

What a thing, he thought—what a thing it is to have meat and be warm and have a full belly. What a thing of joy.

And he slept.

And while he slept he had a dream.

Chapter 7

The Dream

There were swirls of fog like steam off the water in the ice leads; thick fog, heavy fog, that would start to clear and close again, then clear a little more until finally he could see, could see, could see . . .

A skin shelter, a tent, on the side of the ocean. Inside there was an oil lamp, much like the one Oogruk had, burning a smoky yellow that lighted the faces of the people in the tent.

Two children were there. Small and round and wonderfully fat. They were eating of some fat red meat that Russel could not understand, didn't know, but knew as being important. He wanted to know what kind of meat they were eating because it was so red and had coarse texture and rich yellow fat. All over the children's faces and in their hair the grease shone and they were happy with it.

On the other side of the lamp sat a woman, young, round and shining beautiful. She was fat and had eaten of the meat but was done now and worked at tending the lamp. There was much honor in tending the lamp and she took pride in it. The flame was even, if smoky, and in the stone lamp-bowl there was the same yellow fat that was so important for him to name.

One other person was in the skin tent and he couldn't see who it was; it was a man, but he kept back in the shadows and would not come forward.

They were saying nothing, but the children laughed until the laughter was like a kind of music in the background and the woman looked at the man and smiled often. It was the kind of smile all men look for in women, the kind that reaches inside, and Russel felt warm to see it.

But he could not see the man and he did not know the meat, and they were important to him.

The fog came again, and this time when it cleared the man was standing near the doorway in a parka. The parka was deerskin and he held a long spear with some form of black stone point, chipped black stone that was deep and shining dark. He was going out hunting and Russel knew, sensed, that he was going to hunt whatever had made the coarse meat and yellow fat and Russel wanted to go with him.

The woman kept smiling and the children kept laughing but the woman was worried and said something in a language that Russel could not understand. It was words, and they were similar to what he knew, but enough different so they didn't quite make sense to him.

As the man turned to leave the hut the woman said something to him and he stopped and looked at her.

Her eyes glowed at him and there was much fear in them, so much that Russel was afraid, and he knew that there was some fear in the man, too, but hidden.

Russel would not have known that except that he felt close to the man. More than close somehow.

The man left the tent and went out to harness dogs and they were already in harness, waiting for him, and they were dogs but they were more than dogs, too.

Great gray sides twitching, they stood like shadows, with wide heads and heavy triangular jaws. Russel had never seen anything like the dogs in the dream. They were higher than the man's waist and had silent yellow eyes that watched everything the man did while he put his gear in the sled and got ready to leave, and the way they watched it was clear that they could either run or turn and eat him. It was up to the man.

He stood to the sled and Russel saw then that it was not of wood but all of bone and ivory, with large rib bones for the runners, and lashed with yellow rawhide. It shone yellow-white and rich in the night light, the color deep and alive, and when the man stepped on the runners the dogs lunged silently but with great speed and power and the fog closed again, swirled in thick and deep.

When it lifted the man was alone out on the sweeps. The stretch of land looked familiar, but there was something different in the dream and after a time Russel could see that it was the grass. Where the snow had been blown away the grass was taller and thinner, with pointed ends. It was bent over in wind, but not twisted like the tundra grass.

There was deeper darkness now and Russel watched as the man worked the dogs without making a sound. They were clearly hunting something, that much was sure, but what they were hunting Russel couldn't tell. He was amazed to see the man handle the dogs with no audible commands.

They ran to his mind, clean and simple. They went out into the sweeps and Russel watched as if from somewhere above, watched as they hunted in and out of the fog until finally, in a clearing, they found the fresh tracks of whatever they were hunting.

The gray dogs put their hair up and ran to the tracks nervously. They wanted to catch the smell but they didn't want to as well. They were still running to the man's mind and he made them follow the tracks but there was fear now.

Great fear.

The tracks were blurred, but huge, and Russel couldn't see what might have made them. He had never seen tracks like them, nor felt the fear that was in the man.

Then there was a shape before him and Russel fought to see it.

Some great thing it was, some great shape in the fog and then the mist was whirled away in a rush of wind and Russel saw two things clearly.

The animal was a woolly mammoth. Immense, it stood with shaggy hair, its giant domed head swaying, its great tusks curved toward the dogs. The small trunk whipped back and forth in anger and the red eyes tore through the fog like a demon's from the Below World.

The man was to kill the beast if he could, or the beast was to kill the man and the dogs, drive them into the snow and kill them.

That much Russel saw clearly and one more thing.

As the man grabbed the long killing-lance and jumped from the ivory and bone sled, the wind blew off his parka hood and Russel saw the man's face and knew it.

The man was him: Russel, with more hair, longer hair, and a small beard and mustache, but he was Russel and Russel knew fear, deep fear, because with the knowledge that he was the man in the dream he knew that he would have to fight the mammoth. He would have to fight it and kill it.

And the mammoth charged.

The head and tusks thrashed in angry arcs and the huge feet trampled the earth, tearing up clods of dirty snow, as the mighty animal bore down on the man and the dogs and sled.

There was no time for escape, no time for dodging. The man had to face the beast.

The dogs ran to the side, but turned back in as the mammoth rushed by them, heading for the man. But their action caused the animal to swing its head slightly to the side and that revealed the center of the chest.

Crouching and turned away, the man set the shaft of the long lance in the earth and snow in back of him, settled it in as hard as he could and rose to face the oncoming mammoth. With its head sideways to lash at the dogs it roared down on the man as with small arm movements he guided the point of the lance into the center of the chest and let the weight of the animal carry it down the shaft to death.

The lance entered like light, like a beam of light shot into the mammoth and when there should have been death the animal instead wheeled and heaved in a great circle, caught the dogs and threw two of them in the air.

All in silence.

And then the beast stopped. It stood with its head hanging, swaying back and forth, and accepted the death from the broken lance shaft in its chest and went down on its front knees and then its back and in an almost gentle roll slipped to its side and died.

And the man as he saw the animal falter began to sing. Again Russel did not know the words but they sounded familiar to him.

The man sang in exultation.

Sang the death of the great beast, and the mountain of meat lying before him.

Sang the luck of his hunt.

Sang of the fat that would be his for his family and the dogs that now tore at the belly of the mammoth.

Sang the wind that brought his dogs to the tracks and sang the gratitude for the great animal who died and left him much meat.

And Russel felt all those songs inside his soul, felt them even as the man in the dream sang and the fog came again to hide him and the dogs and the mammoth.

Russel knew it all because he knew them all. He was the man and he was the dream.

He was the fog.

Chapter

The Run

The light filtered into the skins and he awakened. Some of the dream was still with him and he had a great hunger for the coarse red meat and yellow fat but when he looked out from the skins he saw only the four deer carcasses. The team was chewing on one.

He stuck an arm out and scraped his parka and turned it right side out and put it on. The cold of the skin penetrated his squirrelskin undergarment and brought him totally, instantly wide awake.

Next he put his mukluks on—they were warm from being in the skins all night—and then he threw back the skins and stood.

The dogs had fought while he dreamed and the gangline was bitten in two or three places. He swore and pulled them back from the deer and to the sled and tied them in place, liberally slamming their noses with his mittened hand.

In a few moments they had settled and he went back to the deer. Their bodies had frozen but were small enough to fit roughly on the sled. Legs stuck out but he wanted to keep going and the legs didn't bother him. There were no trees to catch at them.

The skins were more of a problem. Though he had slept in them the raw sides had frozen solid. The hollow hairs had kept his body heat from penetrating the skins and they would not fold. He finally jumped on them in the middle to fold them over and jam-fit them next to the deer carcasses on the sled.

He pulled his hood on, tightened it against the coming wind and called the dogs up. In minutes he was out of sight of the camp area, heading still north. Out. Into the sweeps.

Today was different—as Russel knew all days are different in the north. It was so cold his spit bounced—white men would call it forty below zero—and the air caught in his throat as he warmed it.

The color was new as well. Yesterday had been blue. Today was almost a deep purple with stringers of clouds shooting across the dimly lighted sky, fingers aimed away from an advancing storm.

Russel knew weather as all Eskimos know weather. The storm would come in two days, maybe a little less, but it would not be too bad. Some wind and cold, nothing more. He could ride it out easily.

But there was a strange unease driving him and at first he thought it was the dream. It had been so real-seeming. He could still smell the inside of the dreamigloo-tent, the stink of the mammoth voiding itself in death, the heat of its blood down the shaft of the lance.

He had killed the beast and yet something was pushing him, making him drive the team. They were new now, a new team. It wasn't that the dogs had changed; and yet they were not the same dogs that he'd first seen at Oogruk's. They changed with him, or at least so it seemed, changed with his mind.

It was as if they had gone out of themselves and become more than dogs, more than animal.

They ran to his mind, out and out before him. With bellies full of deer meat, rich guts and stomach linings, the dogs were strong and driving, had great power, and wanted to run.

He let them run and they seemed to want to head the same way he wanted to go and that, too, became part of his thinking.

Did they know him?

Did they know his mind and run to it the way the wolf-dogs had run to the man's mind in the dream?

And if that were so, which he believed since he seemed to see his thoughts going out ahead, with the lead dog—if that were so, did the dogs know where they were going? Did they know when he didn't know?

And more, did they know *why* they were heading north?

"Why do we run?" he asked aloud and the sudden words broke the silence and startled the dogs. They kept running but broke stride for a few steps before regaining rhythm.

They did not answer.

Twice he looked back but saw nothing and after that he didn't look to the rear again. Out ahead was everything, out ahead was where they were going and he let the dogs decide because that was the same as his deciding.

The snow was right for speed, didn't have the cold-weather scrubbing sound it sometimes did which pulled at the runners, and they ran the daylight out without losing pace.

For five, maybe six, hours he let them run and as the gray dusk was gathering before dark he saw off to the right a small valley between two hills where there was some brush which might make a fire.

He said nothing to the team but they knew and they curved off to the right to head for the valley. There was still light as they came to it. He stopped them near some dried brush, dead in the wind and snow, but the dogs kept pulling forward and he let them go again. Further up there was an overhanging ledge of stone, a shelf, with a place under it to make a shelter. The dogs stopped when they reached the overhang.

He used one skin to shield the opening and scraped enough snow to secure it to the ledge. Then he cut a set of front shoulders up and threw the pieces to the dogs and pulled a second carcass into the lean-to. With the other skins he fashioned a bed and went out and collected bits of brushwood until he had enough to last the night and a little extra.

It was a perfect camp.

He brought the wood into the shelter and pulled the flap down. Using a bit of moss he started a small fire and in moments it was warm inside the shelter. He took his parka off and turned it inside out and put it back outside to freeze.

He heard the dogs growl, but they settled the problem immediately and he turned to warming meat to eat. Using the point of his knife he pried a tenderloin off the middle back of the carcass and held it over the small flame. The smoke was bad at first but he opened a hole at the top of the lean-to and the smoke was quickly sucked out by the wind.

The meat thawed in the flame and was soon warm enough to eat and he put the piece in his mouth and cut it off by his lips.

He was thirsty and he ate more snow with the meat, alternately chewing meat and eating snow until his stomach started to bulge.

He could eat no more yet he was hungry still. He thought of the red coarse meat of the dream, of the rich yellow fat and he closed his eyes.

But there was not sleep at first. Instead he thought of the day's run, then thought of Oogruk asking if they ran for him. It was a pleasant thought and Russel lay back on the hide to rest—but there was a lump beneath his shoulder. He was about to ignore it, to leave it there, but it was such a perfect camp that he wanted the bed to be perfect as well and he folded the skin back to see what the lump was. There was a stone there, a curved piece of stone, and when he pulled at it, it wiggled a bit.

He took his knife and dug around the edge, pulled at it, loosened it more, then dug again. Finally it came free and when it was in his hand he saw that it was more than a stone. It was a stone that had been worked by hand.

It was round, a disc about ten inches in diameter, and smoothly polished. On one side it was completely flat, but on the other it had been hollowed out to form a six inch dish, one edge of which had a small groove in it.

It was an old stone lamp. Older, much older than Oogruk's. Older than the lamps in the museums he had seen that were dug by the college people from the old village up north. Somebody had camped here many years before and either left the lamp or had come upon a disaster which ended what they had been. Only the lamp was left, and Russel held it and wondered at the shiny smoothness of it, the polished beauty.

"See what a man has been given," he said. "By the dogs who brought me. By the night. See what a man has been given." He had dropped into the third person usage without thinking, though it was no longer used very much. He had heard the old people talk that way sometimes out of politeness.

He used the back of his knife to scrape the last of the dirt off the lamp and set it aside. He needed some fat to light it and he went outside once more to the caribou carcass to get stomach fat.

"The best fat to eat is the best fat to burn," Oogruk had said. "Save the best for the flame and you will never be cold. It is a good lesson for a man. Save the best for the flame."

Russel took the stomach fat, pried it off with his knife—it was still frozen—and cut it in chips for the lamp bowl. When he had a small mound of chips he found some moss near the ledge and fashioned a wick. Then he took a burning stick from the fire and tried to light the lamp.

It was necessary to melt the fat into a puddle in the lamp so that as a liquid it could be wicked-up into the moss for burning.

After a good hour of moving the chips around and becoming frustrated he was ready to give up. But he tried once more and was rewarded when the chips of white fat suddenly became fluid and soaked into the moss. Smiling, he lit the wick and set the lamp on a small dirt ledge to the side of the shelter.

The fire died to embers but the lamp glow remained and the sweet yellow of the burning fat kept the night away, kept him warm. The fat was poor, he knew, compared to walrus fat or seal oil. And it burned with some smoke, though much less than the wood fire. But he did not need wood now, as long as he had deer for the fat. And there were many deer.

He could get everything from the deer.

He was sleepy now, again full and round with heat and food. But he didn't know how long the fat would last, or the wick, so he went outside and spent some time getting more fat from the same carcass. When he had a fair small pile of it, cut in chips, he found some more moss and twisted it into wick for later.

He added some chips to the liquid in the bowl and they melted and he saw that it was easy now to keep the level of the liquid up to the edge. Small crackles of rendered fat floated there and with quick fingers he dipped them out and ate them as they cooled.

He took a thin piece of wood and made a scrape-tool to keep the wick even. Then he lay back on the skins as the storm came up and he looked to all he had done and knew Oogruk would have liked it. Where there had been nothing he now had shelter and food and heat and comfort. Where there had been nothing he had become something.

The dogs were fed and down for rest, fed on meat and fat, fed on running and cold, fed and down.

He could sleep now. He would awaken in the night at intervals to add chips of fat to the lamp or to trim the wick, or perhaps to warm and eat a piece of meat or open a leg bone to get at the marrow, which tasted like the butter at the village store, or swallow a bit of snow when thirst took him.

He could sleep now.

And dream.

Chapter 9

The Dream

Here now was a village.

The man drove his dogs out of the fog, the great gray dogs out of the gray fog, as if the dogs were not animals but fog that had come alive. Out they came onto a clearing on top of a bluff overlooking a coastal village, and the man set his bone snowhook.

There were many skin tents along the beach-ice, each tent by a meat rack filled with black blood-meat from walrus and seal. Steam from the heat was coming from the breathing holes on the tents, and though it was dim he saw children playing with puppies near the tents. It was a good camp. All the puppies were fat, and the dogs had good hair and were fat.

In the dream Russel could see over the man, could see how his mind was working and he knew that the man was holding back above the village out of sadness.

The camp was nothing he knew but the playing children and the sounds of women calling to each other through the tent walls made him think of the family he had left when he'd gone to hunt.

He was in a new land but the people were known to him as all people are known to all other people and their words made him think of his own family and he missed them, and for a moment Russel thought he might turn the team and head for home with the red meat and yellow fat.

But the dogs were excited and they jerked the snowhook free and tore down the hill with the ivory and bone sled flying behind like a feather in the wind. They wanted to meet the new dogs and perhaps fight and breed and eat and rest and they pulled the man down into the settlement on the beach.

Everybody came running out of the tents, half-dressed, yelling at the dogs to stop them from fighting, for the man's dogs were among the loose village dogs, snapping and barking, the sled behind them. After much whipping and yelling the dogs were separated.

There was great joy in the village. Visitors came very seldom and strangers almost never. The man had come from far away—they knew that from his dogs which were of a strange bloodline—and he was surely a mighty hunter because his sled was full of meat and his dogs were sleek and well fed even though they had come a long distance.

The new man would have stories to tell, wonderful stories of taking the large beast and traveling through strange lands. They would show the stranger their hospitality by feeding him much fat meat and feeding his dogs until they threw the meat up to eat it again.

Then they would take him into the main tent and they would talk and talk and perhaps later they would sing and dance to the drum and make up songs. Perhaps the stranger would sing his song.

It would be a night to last many days, with eating and eating until nothing more could be put down. A great time.

A new folding.

When it cleared Russel was inside a great tent. There were many people in the tent, sitting around the outside in a circle with the women back on a ledge.

There were a dozen or so lamps burning so that their light made the tent bright, hot-yellow with hazy smoke, and in the middle of the tent with his back to Russel stood the man who had come on the sled with the great gray dogs.

He wore only a breechclout held by a thin leather thong and Russel could see the knotted muscles in his back and down his legs, cords of power. His skin shone with sweat and grease from rubbing his hands on his body to clean them while he ate and his hair hung down in straight lines, heavy with grease.

He is not a man standing on the ground, Russel thought—he is growing up *from* the ground. His legs are the earth and they take strength from it, up through his ankles and into his muscles so that he grows with what he takes from it. More than strength, more than substance—all that the man would be is growing up from the earth through his legs and into his body.

Strong.

Strong beyond what he was merely, the man had grown strong from the dogs and the wind and the winter and strong from the people around in a circle who watched now, watched and waited.

The man kept his back to Russel but Russel knew why and didn't care. He knew that he was the man, knew it and let that knowledge carry him into the man.

And now the man started to move.

His legs shuffled and his head swung from side to side and his hair moved with his body and he was not a man anymore.

He was the mammoth. It was more than a dance, more than a story, he *became* the mammoth, down to the smell, the foul smell that came from the beast.

The man moved and the mammoth moved and the people swept back to avoid being trampled, moved back in fear and some children who had no manners cried out in fear that the beast would see them.

But there was sadness here. For the mammoth knew that he must die, knew that he must furnish meat for the man. And so he knew he must run down the lance and give his death for food. There was sadness in his dance. In his movement.

The man sang and Russel could not understand the words but he knew their meaning: it was the song of the beast, the mammoth's song as he moved to his death at the hands of the puny man with the dogs. It was a noble song, a song to proclaim that he did not really have to die but chose to because it was his time and he would die with rightness, die correctly.

Sadness.

A rich sadness that took the man and made everybody watching feel deeply for the plight of the mammoth, cursed to death to make meat.

But now there was something new.

Now the mammoth grew, took strength and rage. Around the circle the man moved-danced, his voice growing through the song of the mammoth as it first saw the dogs and man.

And in the way of such things it had to attack. There was no sense to it because the mammoth could have kept going away. But the beast turned. In rage it attacked the dogs and turned its head to hit them and ran upon the lance.

Sometimes a man would be wrong and the lance would miss or hit the shoulder and slide off to the side and the man would die, would be trampled to death. Then it was not the time for the mammoth to die but time for the man to die and Russel knew this, knew all of this because of the movements of the man in the dream.

Now he changed again and now he was himself, the man, dancing and moving to kill the mammoth.

And now the beast charged.

And now he ran on the lance.

And now he died.

And it was all in the man and all in the people who watched and all in the small space in the council tent, all of it.

When the song was done the children screamed for joy and hunger at the meat he had brought and the men nodded and grunted approval at his mighty hunting and the women moved for him to attract his eye, because he was a hunter of such stature.

The man fell to the floor exhausted and they left him there, at the side, while somebody else rose to dance his song of a kayak and a walrus and near-death in the water.

And when he was done another got up, and then another, and so the songs soared on and on through day and night as the dream folded back into the fog.

10

The Run

When the storm hit his shelter it awakened him and he listened for a time. But he was secure and had fat for the lamp and he went back to sleep—the best way to ride storms out in the arctic.

When he awakened the next time—perhaps twenty hours later—he was ravenous and thirsty, and outside it was still. He looked from the shelter and saw that the dogs were still sleeping, resting, and would remain so until he called them up. He was learning. If they worked hard they might sleep for three days, getting up just to relieve themselves and change position—not even that if the wind was bad and they had good snow caves made for shelter.

Russel took snow in and ate from it, mourning once more his lack of a pot for cooking and boiling and making water from the snow. He fashioned a ladle from a leg bone but got only sips for his work.

He added fat chips to the lamp, which was halfway empty, and they melted and he found that by pushing the wick further into the fluid fat the flame rose.

He used the expanded flame to heat a piece of loin from the deer and when it was warm ate it in large mouthfuls.

It didn't fill him and he ate some warm fat, then more meat and yet more fat until his stomach bulged and he was again full.

But this time sleep didn't come. He had slept the better part of two days now and no part of his body was tired enough to sleep more.

He looked out of the tent again and saw that daylight was coming.

He shrugged away the camp as he would shrug away light snow. It was time to leave, time to head north again to see the father of ice. He brought his parka in, brushed off the frozen sweat and put it on. Then he pinched the flame out with his fingers and slide his mukluks on and stepped into the darkness. It took him just a few moments to take down the skins, softened now from the heat of the lamp, and fold them in the sled bottom, then the lamp in the sled bag, and finally the rest of the meat on top of the skins and, lastly, his weapons: the lance and harpoon shafts on top of the skins, then his bow and the quiver of arrows. None of the deer had broken arrows when they fell and he had cleaned the points of the bubbled blood that comes from a kill and put them back in the quiver.

Still the dogs weren't moving.

When everything was lashed down to the sled, Russel went up the line and jerked the team out of the snow.

Two of them growled and he slapped them with a mitten across their noses to get their attention.

When they were all up and standing he got on the sled and called them up.

They started slowly, two of them holding back

until he yelled at them again. Then they went to work and headed away from the camp.

Light came gently, but the sky was clear and cold and clean and he let the dogs seek their own pace. Once they had shaken out their legs they began an easy lope that covered miles at a fierce clip.

They ran into light, then all through the day, easily pulling the sled on the fast snow, grabbing a mouthful when they got thirsty, and Russel watched the new country come.

There were few hills now. The land was very flat, and there were no trees of any kind. If he kept going this way for a long time—he was not sure how long it would take with dogs but it took all day with an airplane—he would come to mountains. He thought.

But before the mountains he believed the sea came back in again. In the school he had seen a map that showed the sea coming back into the land but he was not sure if that was straight north or north and west and he was not sure how long it would take to get to the sea by dog sled. He did not know how far dogs traveled in a day.

Yet it didn't matter.

Oogruk had said, "It isn't the destination that counts. It is the journey. That is what life is. A journey. Make it the right way and you will fill it correctly with days. Pay attention to the journey."

So Russel ran the team and now the land was so flat that it seemed to rise around him like a great lamp bowl sloping up to the sky.

Looking ahead, he could feel a small grit coming to his eyes, sensed the first stages of snow blindness—caused when the light comes from all directions, from the white snow and the flat blue sky. When it is very bad it's as if someone has poured sand in the eyes and it's impossible to open them to see. More often snow blindness just irritates.

Russel rubbed his eyes. He knew if he had wood he could make a pair of snow goggles, with small slits to cut out the light from the sides. But he didn't have wood, so he rubbed his eyes now and then and pulled his hood tighter.

When the short day was gone the dogs didn't seem to want to stop. He let them run. There was no place to camp anyway and his mind looked now to the run.

He had come north a long way but was not sure how long. In the dark they kept up the pace, increased it, and they could cover many more miles before he had to rest them again, running on fresh meat as they were.

He sensed in the night that he was passing a large herd of deer and the dogs started for them but he had meat and called them back to the north. They obeyed instantly and he felt good.

They were his now. They were his dogs and they would run to him. He made the meat for them and they would run to him—just as the dogs in the dream ran to the man. Just as they ran, his dogs would run.

Out into the night he ran, and through the other side of darkness.

It was coming into first light when he saw the snowmachine tracks.

They started as if by magic. Suddenly the snow bore the small ridges that come from a snowmachine.

They headed off to the north.

The dogs dropped into the line of the tracks easily, as they dropped into any trail, which surprised Russel. Given a chance they seemed to follow the path of least resistance as if they expected something.

Russel let them run and thought for a time. He knew quite an area, had once flown to a northern settlement, a village three hundred miles up the coast from his own.

But he could not think of a settlement that fit with the tracks. There was nothing straight north. If the tracks were a hunting party from the village, it was way out of the normal hunting territory—and besides, Russel thought, anybody hunting now would be working the sea ice for seals.

He did not want to see anybody, especially somebody on a snowmachine. The idea of a snowmachine was out of place, opposite, wrong.

But.

It was possible that whoever it was might have an extra pot or can he could use. He sorely missed having a way to boil meat or make water from snow and his lips were starting to crack and bleed from the snow's sharpness. If he did not find a way to melt snow his lips would soon go to sores.

Oogruk had talked of using stone bowls to melt snow but Russel couldn't find the right kind of soft stone and so he hoped to find a pot or a can.

And there was the other thing. He was starting to notice the dogs, notice that they seemed to be an extension of his thoughts. Now they ran to the trail and perhaps that was because he wanted them to run to the trail.

Perhaps he wanted to see whoever it was, see where the tracks led. So he let them run the snowmachine trail and they lasted through that day and into the night and still he ran. The tracks led steadily to the north, the line moving out to the rim of the white saucer into dark and then out of sight into the blackness.

Always north.

He let the dogs run, stopping in the cold dawn to feed them some meat, taking a cold mouthful for himself, then eating some snow, wincing in pain from his cracked lips, and moving them on.

He saw no game that day, no other sign but the snowmachine tracks with the slight dusting of snow on the edges, filling in as the wind blew, and he debated stopping.

But the dogs wanted to run and he let them.

They ran the second night, and he did not sleep but his mind circled and slipped down as he rode the runners, tired but not tired. He quit thinking, quit being anything but part of the sled, part of the dogs. At one time he began to hallucinate and thought somebody was riding the sled in front of him, sitting in the basket. A blurred idea of someone.

But then the hallucination was gone and another one came; he saw lights on all the dogs' feet, small lights, and then they disappeared and he felt somehow that the opening of his parka hood was a mirror and everything he saw in front of him was somehow in back of him, and then, driving on into the night, the mirror vanished and he had the dream.

The dream again.

But darker.

Chapter 11

The Dream

The man was no longer in the settlement on the edge of the sea, fat with walrus and seal oil, among fat puppies and round dogs and round faces.

Now there was not a fog, but a slashing gray storm that took everything.

He was trying to drive his dogs in the storm and there was an air of madness to it. The wind tore at them, lifted their hair and drove the snow underneath it to freeze on their skin until the dogs were coated in ice. Icedogs. They shone through the snow as they tried to drive forward.

But the wind tore at them. The dogs were blown sideways so hard that they leaned to stand and when they hit patches of ice or frozen snow they went down, staggering.

Yet the man drove them.

He stood on the runners, screamed blindly at them, let the long whip go out to tear at their flanks. His will flew along the line to the dogs, pushing them fiercely into the roaring storm.

Russel could see no sense to it. The sled was full of

the red meat, the man could stop and make a shelter and eat and feed the dogs and wait for the storm.

But there was terrible worry in the man, fear and worry that Russel could feel, up from the dream into his mind, into his soul, and when he let his mind go into the dream, into the man, he knew the reason.

He had stayed long at the village with the fat of seal and walrus. Perhaps too long. And now the journey home was taking too long, too long for the family that waited back in the skin tent for the red meat and fat.

The storm was stopping him. He could fight and fight, whip the dogs until they ran red with blood, but the storm was stopping him.

It was too fierce. Now it blew the dogs sideways, and now it blew them backward and they felt the frustration of the man and it became anger and they fought among themselves, tearing and slashing.

The man used his whip handle like a club and beat them apart and settled them and admitted defeat, fell in the wind, fell next to the sled and huddled in his parka as the gray blasts of snow took him down and down . . .

The wind took the dream with snow as the fog had once taken it, closed on it. But now the dream wasn't finished . . .

From Russel's mind came the tent with the woman and the two children. But now they were not the same . . . Now the lamp flickers with the last of the oil and the faces are thin. Worse than thin, the children's faces have the deep lines and dark shades that come from starvation.

Both children lie quietly on the sleeping bench, end to end, their heads together. They are very weak, weak perhaps beyond coming back.

The mother sits by the lamp, fingering the

strangulation cord. There are no skins left. They have eaten them all. They have eaten all the skin clothing and the soles from their mukluks and the leather lines cut to use for tying dogs.

They have cut the mittens into small squares to chew on the skin, spitting the hair out, and now those are gone.

Everything is gone.

And outside, the storm still tears and rips the earth, drives the snow sideways, guts the land.

She would eat the skin of the tent but that is the same as dying. With the tent gone the wind and cold would have them. They have no clothing left, will have no oil left when the lamp goes out.

Nothing.

The mother is weaker than the children but she takes a finger now and wipes it in the small bit of rancid oil in the lamp and wipes the finger across the lips of each child, leaving a thin film of grease on each lip.

One child licks the grease off.

The other does not.

And outside, the wind slashes and looks for their lives.

The hungry wind.

Chapter 12

The Run

He came upon the snowmachine in the flat white light of the arctic dawn. It was sitting on its skis, just squatting in the middle of the great sweeps.

Nobody was near it. Russel stopped when the dogs were next to it and set his hook. On the back of the seat was a box and he opened it, hoping to find a coffee can or pot but there was nothing but an empty plastic gas jug.

He felt the engine with a bare hand. It was cold, still cold, dead cold.

It was a fairly new machine and while it was true that snowmachines broke down, the newer ones tended to last a bit longer. He opened the gas tank and found it bone dry.

A smile cut his lips and made them bleed.

"They are not of the land," he said to the dogs. "They need fuel that is not part of the land. They cannot run on fat and meat."

A small set of footprints led off ahead of the machine but there were also snowmachine tracks. It was as if another snowmachine had gone ahead, but left the person to walk. It made no sense.

Or. Perhaps the snowmachine had come out this way and the rider was headed back when the machine ran out of gas.

That made more sense to Russel, considering the tracks.

But there was nothing, no village, where the footprints were leading. Nothing that Russel knew about at any rate, and if whoever left the tracks was heading for help on foot he had almost no chance of getting anywhere. There were no settlements within walking distance of the snowmachine.

And the tracks were small enough to belong to a child. Or a girl.

He pulled the hook and the team started off silently. They had run steadily now for two days and needed rest. They could sleep running, a dozesleep, but they needed real rest after the hard work of a long run.

But with the full light Russel could see the high wisps of clouds that meant a storm was coming.

He wanted to try to catch whoever was ahead before the storm hit. On foot he could not be carrying much of a shelter, nor could he be carrying much food. And if it was a child he would probably not survive a bad storm.

Russel let the dogs adopt a slower trot, but he kept them going steadily, watching the tracks ahead.

At first they didn't seem very fresh. The rising wind had blown them in so that some of them were filled completely. But as the hours passed they seemed to be getting cleaner, newer. Now and then the lead dog dropped his nose to smell them, looking for scent, and Russel could see his ears jerk forward whenever he got a bit.

And when the darkness came again the leader

started to run with his nose down all the time, following the smell of the trail that must be fresh, Russel knew, to hold for the dogs.

But now there was wind and more wind. Not as bad as the dreamwind, but getting worse all the time so that the dogs had to lean slightly left into it to keep their balance. And snow.

There was a driving sharp snow with the wind. Not heavy snow, but small and mean and it worked with the force of the wind to get inside clothing, in the eyes, even blow up into the nostrils.

And finally, when he could no longer see the trail, no longer see the front end of the team, could barely make out the two wheel-dogs directly in front of the sled, finally he came to that time when he should stop and hole up in the storm.

And he did not.

He drove them on. They wanted to stop, twice the leader did stop, but Russel used words as a whip and drove them.

The leader was all important now. The trail was gone, wiped away by the wind and snow in the dark, but the dog sensed with his nose and his feet where the tracks lay and he followed them. Russel almost did not believe the dog could do this—almost, but not quite. Had it happened earlier, when he first started to run the team, back at Oogruk's, he would not have believed. But now he understood more of the dogs, knew that they had understanding he did not have. Yet.

And he believed in the dogs.

The only advantage they had was that the storm was almost straight out of the north. They could fight dead against the wind and that was a bit easier than going side-on where the team would have been blown over.

But it was hard. And the storm, it seemed, worsened by the minute. At length Russel sensed that they were going up a slight incline, not a hill so much as a gradual upgrade, and at the top the dogs stopped dead in the wind.

He yelled at them, swore at them, finally began slamming the sled with his mittened hand and threatened to come up to the unseen dogs and beat them into submission.

But they would not move.

So they are done, he thought. He would have to make a shelter and ride the storm out. But first he would walk to the front of the team and bring the leader back around and use the dogs to form a part of a shelter.

He staggered against the wind to the front of the line and as he reached down for the collar on the lead dog he tripped and fell on something in the trail.

When he had recovered he saw that it was a booted foot, attached to a leg, and by moving up along the leg he found a person with a parka lying curled up, face away from the wind, extremely still.

He shook the figure with his hand but there was no response and he thought the person must be dead.

So much death, he thought. Oogruk and now this person. So much death given in this hard place.

But as he turned away he saw the arm move, or thought he saw some movement, and when he looked back he was sure of it—the bulky form had some life. Somewhere inside the round shape huddled on the trail there was a living person.

There was little time now. Whoever it was, the life was almost gone. There had to be a place to live now, a warm place, and Russel worked as fast as he could without sweating. Sweat, of all things, could kill. Steadily, evenly, he brought the dogs around and placed them down with his hands in a living screen across the face of the wind. They would soon be covered with snow and warm in their small igloos.

Then he took the skins from the sled and using the sled basket as one wall made a tent lean-to of two skins, folding one with the hair in to make a floor. The wind took the tent down twice, pulling the skins out and away so that he had to fight hard to keep them. But at last, using some bits of cord from the sled bag, he tied the skins down at the corners to the sled and packed snow around them and they held. The wind would blow more snow in and pack them still further.

Then he put the lamp and a partial carcass into the lean-to and went back for the figure in the snow. It took much heaving, pulling on the feet, to get the unconscious person into the lean-to and reclose the flap so the wind wouldn't tear it open. But he succeeded at last and fumbled with matches to get the lamp going. It started slowly, casting only a tiny flicker of light, until the fat around the wick began to melt and when it was going at last and he could feel some heat coming from it he turned to his companion.

When he pushed the hood back he was stunned to see that it was a girl. Woman, he thought— girl-woman. She had a round face with the white spots that come from freezing, and pitch-black thick hair pulled back in a bun and held with a leather thong.

He rubbed her cheeks but there was no response and yet he could see that she was breathing. Small spurts of steam came up in the cold yellow air in the lean-to. There was life inside the frozen shell.

He tore off her outerparka. Really it was a light anorak made of canvas, and underneath she had on a vest. When the parka was off he realized that she was not only a young woman but that she was pregnant.

This realization stopped him and he settled back on his haunches to think of it. There were so many strange things here. She was where she couldn't possibly be, riding a snowmachine that had run out of gas, with no supplies, coming from nowhere and going nowhere.

She couldn't be.

And yet she was.

And she was pregnant and nearly dead.

He chipped some pieces of fat off the deer carcass and added them to the lamp. He did it several times while he thought on what to do. Soon the lamp was full of fat and he remembered the dream, remembered the woman trying to save the children from starvation.

He took his finger and dipped it in the fat of the lamp and wiped it across the blue lips. There was no indication from the woman-girl at all. He did it again, and again, until some of the fat had worked into her mouth and then he saw the jaw move. Not a swallowing, not a chewing, but a ripple in the jaw muscle.

She was coming back.

Soon the pain would hit her. When somebody has gotten close to death by freezing and he comes back, Russel knew, there is terrible pain. Sometimes it was possible to relieve the pain by rubbing snow on the frozen parts but when it was the whole body nothing helped.

The pain had to be. It was considered by some— by Oogruk—to be the same pain as birth. To have been close to death and come back could not be done without the pain of birth.

Russel sat back again, then cut some meat and

held it over the flame. After the pain would come hunger. She would want to eat. As he wanted to eat.

The meat softened with the flame and when it had taken on some warmth he ate part of it. Doing so made him think of the dogs and he considered cutting them food but decided to let them sleep for a time first. They had run long and were probably too tired to eat.

Instead he ate some more meat and watched the woman-girl he had rescued. He did not think anything, left his mind blank. There was nothing to think. Just the storm outside and the girl-woman who had almost died but who had come back.

He was extremely tired and as soon as the shelter—drummed into noise by the wind and blown snow—had warmed and the meat had reached his stomach he couldn't hold his eyes open.

He slept sitting up—or didn't sleep so much as close his eyes—and ceased to be in the tent.

His mind slid sideways into the dream.

Chapter 13

The Dream

The storm had cleared but it had taken days, many days. Too many days.

The man got the dogs up, up out of stiffness and the frozen positions they had taken in ice. One got up and fell over, too far gone to live. The man used his spear and the quick thrust to the back of the head to kill the dog. Its feet were frozen and it would have been in agony if he had tried to keep it alive. When it was dead he threw the carcass on the sled to feed the other dogs later.

Then he made them go. They did not want to leave, they were stiff with cold, but he whipped them and made them go.

Across the strange dreamgrass and dreamsnow they moved, the bone and ivory sled starting slow and pulling hard. He stopped and urinated on the runners, using a piece of hide with hair on it to smooth the new ice, and the sled pulled much easier.

And now, where the land had been open and barren, there was much game for the man. He passed herds of caribou, once another mammoth which had died and was frozen, with giant wolves tearing at it.

The wolves watched him pass. Two of them made a small sweep toward the sled and the man—there were times when they would have killed and eaten both the man and the dogs—but there was much easy meat on the mammoth. They turned away without making an open threat but it wouldn't have mattered.

The man almost did not see them. He had one purpose now, driving the lined-out team in front of him. Down to four stiff dogs, but loosening by the mile, he ran them out. The whip cracked and cracked again, reaching out to flick meat from their backs, meat and tufts of hair that flew into the cold, and they ran for him.

They ran for home.

Across the white land they ran, across the whiteness that was so bright in the dream it turned at last into light. Whitelight with the dogs churning through the brightness, legs slamming forward and down, feet kicking up snow, day into night into day into night into day . . .

The dreamdogs ran in the dreamworld across the whitelight until finally in the great distance they disappeared and out in front of what they were, what they had become, Russel could see the space where the tent was in the dream.

But it was the tent space only.

Torn leather, ripped skins that flew and flapped, tattered banners in the never-ending arctic dreamwind.

Where there had been a place of life, a place of laughter and round fat faces, where there had been a place of things that meant home and living, there was only the bleak shreds of flapping leather and the signs of death.

An end to things.

No, Russel thought—out of the dream but still in it in some way he did not understand. No, that cannot be.

But it was. In the dream it was. There was an end that came in the north, an end that came to all things, the same end that came to Oogruk. The wolves had come, and when they were done, the small white foxes had come, and where there had been a woman and two children, where they had ended their lives, there was nothing.

Two bones.

Neither of them was identifiable except as bones, but they were human because they had not been cracked for the marrow and if they had been left from meat the woman would have cracked them to eat the marrow—one small and the other large and long.

Two bones.

They were in the space that used to be tent but they were all. Everything else, every little thing that would have meant life and home was gone.

Even the lamp.

But only a small distance to the north, under an overhanging ledge, the lamp lay. Russel saw it. A fox had taken it there; drawn by the smell of fat that for years had soaked into the stone, it had taken the lamp under the ledge to get away from the other foxes and had licked the fat-smell until even that smell was gone.

Then it had left the lamp and trotted away.

It was a shallow stone lamp, with a flat bottom and a groove in the edge where the moss wick would lie.

The dreamlamp lay where the fox had dropped it, lay until the blowing wind would cover it with snow and the snow would make grass and the grass would cover it still more, and then the snow and grass would, each after the other, time after time, mat the lamp down where it would lie forever. Or until somebody came to move it.

The lamp, Russel dreamthought. Not all that was left . . .

Another shift came; the dream moved sideways once more and he saw the man. Into the night and back to day the man had driven the sled until the dogs were staggering, falling. They were run down so far they would die surely. There would not be a team when the man was done—there would be only dead dogs.

Nothing but the man would be left.

They had run through the light, through the dreamlight the dreamdogs had run until they were no more.

Until there was only the man and the sled and where the tent had been flapping in the wind, only tattered pieces of tent.

And the man was Russel and Russel was the man. He knew that the woman and two children were no more and that the dogs would be no more and that's when Russel awakened in his own tent and saw the lamp.

Saw the flickering lamp and felt himself bathed in the stink-sweat of fear and knew, knew in his center, that it was the same lamp and that it was all there was left of what had been.

That's when Russel awakened in his own tent and knew that there was not a line any longer between the dream and the run.

That's when Russel awakened in his own tent stinking of fear and sweat, knowing that the dream had become his life and his life and the run had become the dream and the woman was looking at him.

The woman-girl, girl-woman sat staring at him past the flickering yellow of the lamp.

And she was the same woman as the woman in the dream. The same round face of the girl-woman in the dream, the same hair, the same even mouth of the dreamwoman-girl, with the same wide nose and clear eyes staring at him through the flamelight.

The dreamflame.

From the dreamlamp.

Chapter 14

The Dreamrun

At the other end of the dreamrun nothing was the same as when he started. At the other end, Russel was no longer young but he wasn't old, either. He wasn't afraid, but he wasn't brave. He wasn't smart, but he wasn't a fool. He wasn't as strong as he would be, but he wasn't ever going to be as weak as he was.

When he thought of what happened, later, when he wasn't what he would be but wasn't what he had been, he thought that in some mysterious way a great folding had happened.

The dream had folded into his life and his life had folded back into the dream so many times that it was not possible for him to find which was real and which was dream.

Nor did he feel that it was important to decide. In its way the dream was more real than the run, than his life.

These things happened. Either in the dream or the run, either in one fold or another fold, these things happened:

He came to know the woman-girl. She was named

Nancy. She had become pregnant without meaning to, without being married, and because the missionaries had told her that it was a sin she had been driven by her mind, driven out into the tundra to die on the snowmachine.

But fear had taken her. She had been afraid to die and she had turned to go back—she did not know how far she had come—and she had run out of gas. She had started to walk, had gone down with the cold, was going to die and Russel saved her.

She had gone first out to sea and then turned inland so they would think she'd gone through the ice and would not look for her inland. She did not have parents to worry for her. Her baby was not due for four months but she had pain in the tent that first night and Russel worried, though there was nothing he could do for her.

They could not leave. The storm was too strong for them to leave. He fed her meat and fat from a caribou carcass, watching her eat and talk between mouthfuls, heating the pieces of meat and putting them in her mouth, holding back when she winced with pain as she came back from freezing, handing her the next piece when she was ready for it. He let her talk and talk, now that he was rested.

When at last she had settled and had stopped talking about herself she stared at him.

"What is the matter?" Russel asked. "Have you never seen people before?"

Nancy looked down, suddenly shy. "It isn't that. It just came to me that you were out here with a dog team. There is nothing out here. How did you come to be here?"

Russel thought of telling her of Oogruk, of the dream, of the run, but held back. That was part of his song and it wouldn't be good to talk about it before it was ready to sing.

Then he thought he might tell her of the lamp, but decided against that for the same reason. Finally he shrugged. "I am a person who is running north and came upon your machine. That is all." He did not tell her about following the tracks for so long.

"How far north?"

It was an impertinent question but he ignored the discourtesy. "Until I run to the end of where I am going."

And then she did a strange thing. She nodded, almost wisely. "I understand. But tell me, is it possible for a person to be with you when you run north to the end?"

It was a hard question to answer. In this run, Russel thought, in this run I thought I would be alone but it was perhaps not supposed to be so. It may be that is what the dream is telling me. That I am not supposed to be alone. If the dream is telling me anything.

Or another way of thinking: Is it possible to leave her out here? No. And still a third way: Would it be possible to take her home?

"There is nothing for me there," she said, shaking her head when he asked. "I have done wrong. There is not a way to live there. I will stay out here."

"And die," Russel finished for her.

"Yes."

"No." He shook his head. "You tried that and it didn't work. You became afraid and tried to get home."

"Not home," she corrected. "Back. I have no home."

"So."

"So."

"What am I to do?"

"Take me with you. I will earn my way. I can scrape the skins and sew them. I can make camp. I can feed dogs."

"Do you know dogs?"

"No. There were none left in my village. But I can learn."

And in that way she came to be with him when his life folded into the dream and the dream folded into his life.

In that way she came to be with him on the run.

Again during that long storm-night she slept and he dozed, but did not dream, and when he awakened this time there was light outside the tent and the wind had stopped. He reached outside and brought his parka in, scraped the ice off, slid it over his underparka and stood outside. He was stiff, worse than he'd ever been, so he stretched, felt his bones crack and creak.

The woman-girl put her anorak on and came out.

"It is cold," she said.

"Cold is our friend."

"I know. But I am not dressed as you. I feel it more."

"We will wrap you in skins in the sled. You will be all right."

She said nothing but nodded and began taking the tent down while he hacked meat off the carcass for the dogs. She put one skin on the bottom of the sled, curved up on the sides, with the hair in. The other three she put on top as a kind of blanket, with the fur inside. When it came time to go—after he had fed and brought the dogs up—she got in between the hides.

"There is comfort here."

He misunderstood. "I have never hauled anybody who is going to have a baby."

"I meant it is warm. There is nothing comfortable

about having a baby."

"Ahh. I see."

The dogs were rested but stiff and it took them a mile or so to loosen up. But they settled into the routine of running; the leader knew that Russel wanted to cover distance and they ran.

The land was new. White-new with snow from the storm and drifts from the wind and after a time the dogs were running up the sides of a white saucer into the light, running out and out until their legs vanished in light and the steam came back to Russel across their backs and turned them into part of the wind, turned them into ghostdogs.

He stood the sled loosely, proud of the team, and he could tell that the woman-girl thought highly of them.

Out, he thought. Out before me they go. Out before me I go, they go . . .

They ran north, now two where there was one, ran north for the mother of wind and the father of ice.

And these things happened when Russel's life folded into the dream and the dream folded into his life:

It came that they ran past their food.

It was true that he perhaps fed the dogs a bit too much, but they were working hard and it took meat and fat to drive them. Three, four, seven more days of running north, stopping at night in the skins with the lamp and the chips of fat and the yellow glow while they ate much and talked little; sat in their own minds until they dozed and he came to know the woman-girl—eight, nine, ten days and nights they ran north toward the mother of wind, and they ran past their food.

The first and second day without food there was

no trouble. The dogs grew weak, but when they didn't get fed they went back to work and began to use of the stored fat and meat of their bodies.

"They will run to death," Oogruk had said. "You must not let them."

At the end of the second day Russel's stomach demanded food and when he didn't feed it and ignored it his body finally quit asking for food and he went to work and began using the meat and fat of his body.

The woman-girl grew weak rapidly because her body fed the baby within. Russel saved the last of the food for her and when that was gone and it was obvious that the dogs could not go much further he stopped.

There had been no game. No sign. They had seen nothing and he was worried. No, more than worried—he had been worried when the first two days with no game sighted had come. Now he was afraid.

He had to make meat.

"I will leave you in the tent and take the team for meat. They will run lighter with only one person."

Nancy agreed, nodding. She got slowly out of the sled and pulled the skins out to make the shelter. They were near the side of a cut bank where a creek had long ago run. They used the dirt bank for one wall and made a lean-to.

There were some chips for the lamp, and a long strip of fat that he had been saving for fuel—pictures from the dream haunted him and he did not want to leave her without heat.

When the shelter was up he returned to the sled. "I'll be back."

It was as close as he would come to a goodbye and he made the dogs leave. They did not want to go.

They thought they should sleep in camp and eat and saw no reason to go out again. But he forced them and when they were away from camp he made them run to the east, up the old creekbed. If there is game, he thought, it will be up the creek run.

But they went all of that day into the dark and he saw nothing. No hare, no ptarmigan, no tracks of anything.

With dark he stopped and lay on the sled in his parka. There was light wind, but not the vicious cold of the previous days of running. He tried to sleep but it did not come.

Instead he lay awake all night thinking of the woman-girl back in the tent. If he did not find game she would die.

She would die.

He would die.

The dogs would die.

Perhaps I ought to run back to her and kill and eat the dogs, he thought, over and over. If he kept running away from the shelter until the dogs went down he would not get back to her. If there was not game out ahead of him he would not get back to her. If he saw game but his mind was not true and the arrow flew wrong he would not get back. She would die.

She would die.

He would die.

The dogs would die.

But if he went back and they ate the dogs they would not be able to leave and they would die anyway.

And now when he thought, there was nothing from the ghost of Oogruk. No help. Nothing. Nothing from the trance or the time when they turned to yellow smoke.

Whatever decision he made, when the light came back, it was *his* decision, just as going back to live the old way must have been *his* decision.

And when the light came across the snow he made the decision to go ahead to find game, knowing that if he was wrong they would all be wrong, the woman-girl, the dogs and all would be wrong and gone. Gone and gone.

In the second day he found nothing. Nor did he on the third day and now they had gone six days without eating and he felt weak. His eyes worked poorly and he ate snow so often that his lips were sore. Twice, then several more times, he thought he saw deer but when he got to where they had been there was nothing. Never had been anything. It was the hunger in his eyes, he found, that made him see things.

Finally the dogs stopped. They could pull no more, or so they thought. But now he remembered one more thing from Oogruk.

"The dogs run because they want to run," the old man had told him, "or because they think *they* want to run, or because you *make* them think they want to run. That is how to drive dogs."

And so now Russel drove them. He cut a whip from some willows in the old streambed and he laid it on their backs and they ran for him but it was wrong, wrong to drive them down that way and he knew that when he had whipped them and made them run and they went down there would be nothing left.

He would not get back to Nancy. His mind took that and made it part of him—he was failing. He would not get back. As in the dream, he would not get back and there would be only two bones left by the foxes.

Two bones.

And so he drove the dogs down, drove them the way the man in the dream had driven them and when his mind was gone, when there was nothing left of his thinking and nothing left of the dogs, he came around a bend in the old streambed and saw tracks.

At first he didn't believe them. They came off the left side of the bank and tore down into the snow at the bottom, breaking through the hard pack that had held the dogs and sled. He thought they were from the hunger in his eyes but when he got closer they did not go away.

They were huge.

And when he got still closer he saw that they were tracks of a great polar bear and that he did not believe, either, because the bear were hunted out for their white fur. Men used snowmachines and hunted them out and there were no bears.

But there were the tracks. And they were tracks of a great bear. And they had to be real because now the dogs caught the smell and took excitement. They increased speed but he knew that they could not last now.

And how to kill a bear?

Oogruk had said nothing.

The arrow would not be enough. He had the killing lance on the sled and he would have to use that somehow. He would have to catch the bear and use the lance to kill it.

A polar bear that was bigger than he, the team, the sled, the woman-girl and the tent combined—he had to take it with the small killing lance in the old way that nobody had used for so long that he didn't think there was a memory of it. Oogruk had never done it, or he would have told him.

The dogs went faster still and he was afraid that he

would burn them out. He stopped them and let the right point dog loose—the one just in back of the leader on the right. He seemed to be the strongest dog and the most excited by the smell of the bear tracks. Perhaps he would catch the bear and keep it busy until Russel could get there and bring it down. Or try.

There was much doubt in him now about the bear, some fear, and more doubt. But the dog tore away up the streambed and Russel took the killing lance from the tie-down on the sled and loosened the bow case and quiver.

Then he let the dogs take the sled after the loose dog. They were clamoring to run—even though weakened by hunger. They smelled it now, saw him take up the weapons and knew that he would try to kill soon and the sight made them crazy.

Up the old stream they wound, following the tracks, faster and faster until at last they came around a corner and there it was.

The bear had his rear back against the bank, his head low and teeth bared. He was immense, the largest bear Russel had ever seen, even in pictures. The fur was dirty white, almost yellow. It was an old male, with his teeth worn down, but full of the winter death that makes a polar bear so awesome. When he saw the sled coming he raised on his hind legs and Russel's heart almost stopped. The bear was a tower, a white-yellow tower standing over the loose dog. The dog had been dodging back and forth, trying to worry the bear, but when the bear raised he went in to bite at the white back leg. It was his last act.

The bear's head snaked down in a great curve of power and his jaws closed on the back of the dog and broke its back in a bite so savage that the dog was dead before it could scream. Then the bear shook its head—a tearing shake—and the dead dog flew sideways in a spray of gore.

All in silence.

But now the bear rumbled in its throat and turned to Russel and the sled and the team. Here was an enemy, a thing to face, and it would face it and kill it.

But wait, Russel thought. But wait, bear. It is the same as the mammoth. There is sadness here for the same reason. A dog is dead. You will want the other dogs and you will turn your head sideways and the lance will enter you like light. But wait, bear. Wait for me. Wait for the sadness of your life that you must die to feed the man. Not all the time. But wait for the sadness this time, bear.

Russel took the lance and stood away from the sled and let the dogs go. They went for the bear in a pummeling scream, and with the same sharp movement the bear lowered on all fours and came for Russel.

The bear did not want the dogs. He wanted Russel. He wanted to kill the enemy standing with the little stick, kill the man. Kill the man-thing.

Russel felt a great calmness. He wasn't Russel. He was the man in the dream and the bear wasn't a bear but the great stinking beast and Russel set the shaft of the killing lance in the ground and held the wide-ivory point at the right height to take the bear at the base of his throat and now the bear came and now the dogs swerved in to take him and the bear's head went sideways for the dogs and the bear, stinking with the same smell as the beast in the dream, and now the bear had his head sideways and now the lance entered.

Like light. It slid through the hair and the fat and

into the center of the bear, into the center of the center of the bear and Russel screamed a savage roar of triumph and the bear was on him.

On him and over him, hitting him with a stunning blow of his right paw even as the lance took his life. Russel knew he had killed the bear, but felt the pain and saw the flash as his own life seemed to fly from him and he thought with a violent clarity: but wait, bear.

But wait, bear.

And then he saw nothing.

And these things happened when Russel's life folded into the dream and the dream folded into his life:

When he came back into his life from where the bear had knocked him away the bear was dead and the dogs were chewing at his rear end and Russel was underneath his left front shoulder, the blood dripping down on him from where the lance shaft had entered the bear.

He fought to get from under and crawl to the side. When he could stand, his head aching and dizzy, he looked down on the bear and felt his heart go out of him and into the bear.

"Thank you. The meat will be welcome."

A sadness took him, because he had no food for the bear. Such a bear it was, so big, but he had nothing for him but the thought of food. It would have to be enough.

The bear was a mountain of meat. It weighed close to three quarters of a ton. More meat than he could eat, than the dogs could eat in a month. More even than the woman-girl . . .

He remembered her suddenly.

He would feed the dogs and take some meat and

go back for her. As fast as possible.

He used his knife to lift the back-end hide and took a large chunk of meat from the rear leg. This he fed to the dogs, who ate and puked and ate again. Then he took another large chunk of fat meat, which he put in the sled, and he turned them and started back.

They didn't want to leave the bear. The meat had given them strength almost miraculously fast, but they didn't want to leave the kill. He finally had to get in front and drag the leader back down the streambed until they had gone around two bends and were well away from the dead bear. Even then they worked reluctantly for a time.

But he let them seek their own pace and kept them going and in two days—feeding them liberally from the meat as he drove them—they had come within sight of the tent.

It was day—clear and cold—and he saw the lean-to half a mile before they got to it. It was not tattered, but there was not steam coming from the opening at the top and he feared for her.

"Nancy!" He called her name when he came near the tent. "I am back . . ."

But there was no answer. He set the hook and grabbed the meat and ran for the tent. It took him just a second to lift a corner and get inside but he felt the cold immediately.

She was lying on her side, the end of a skin wrapped around her as a sleeping bag and she was either sleeping or dead or in a coma.

The lamp was out. The fat was gone. He took some from the bear, rich yellow fat, and cut pieces into the lamp. He found some moss and got the lamp going—as the first time, only with great difficulty.

The warmth came out from the flame at once and

he opened the skin around the woman-girl to let the heat reach her.

When he moved her he saw her eye flicker and he thought: twice. Twice she has come back from death.

But this time she was not frozen, as she had been the first time, or not frozen to such depth. There was not that wrong with her. She smiled at him.

"I did not think you were coming back." She spoke in a whisper that was almost a hiss.

"I said I would be back."

She said nothing more. He cut meat in small pieces and heated them on the lamp and put them in her mouth and she chewed and swallowed and where there had been an end there was once more a beginning.

But worse was wrong. Worse than he thought could be.

Even with the meat she did not revive. She ate, but when he thought she should eat more she held back and she did not come up and because he had come to know the woman-girl he worried.

"You are sick," he said. Outside it was dark and the wind was blowing again. Or still. "What makes you sick?"

She didn't answer at first. Then she grunted. "It is the baby. The baby is coming early. I cannot stop it."

"Ahh. That is not good, is it?"

"No." She turned away from him, face to the back of the tent. "Maybe you should leave me alone."

But he had run once, left her to go for meat and he would not leave her again. Leaving had torn him and he still thought of the dream and the tattered tent with the foxes. "I will stay."

She said nothing to this and he took that as acceptance—or perhaps she was too sick to argue.

"Is there a thing I can do?" he asked.

But again she did not answer. He put more fat in the lamp, pulled the wick up to make more heat, then went outside and fed the dogs. They would sleep for days now, he knew, and that was fine. He had enough meat to last a long time and by then they would be able to travel. If not, he could just go back to the carcass and get more. With a strong team it was only a day and a half away.

With food anything was possible.

When the dogs were fed and the meat pulled back in the shelter, he felt the exhaustion come down on him and it was not possible for him to stay awake.

In the warmth of the lean-to he slept, the ringing, deep sleep of the utterly tired when it seems as if nothing can awaken the mind. His head lay back against her feet and he slept and thought he would not dream.

But a thing came. He could not say if it was a dream or if it was real. But a thing came to happen in that night that he knew—and if he knew it sleeping or knew it awake it did not matter.

Foldings:

The woman-girl became a woman in the night. She was quiet at first, but moving and throwing her body back and forth and then in the yellow of the lamp she gave short-sharp sounds, sounds from the center of her center.

And he saw-felt that.

She strained and heaved and pushed and in the folds of the skin and the agony of it was not something he understood but he knew the sadness because it was the same sadness somehow that killing the bear had been.

In his mind he tried to help her but he was not sure if he really did or only wished that he could.

And still she worked. The cries became closer

together, and shorter, and deeper, and then she screamed, and then a time, a lifetime of almost animal whimpers and another scream and the thing had happened and it was in his hands and there was not life in it.

"Take it away!" she screamed. "Take it away now. Before I see it. Put it away from me. Outside."

And either he did or dreamed he did or wished he did—he went from the tent with the baby and up on the hill in back of the tent and he walked in the cold and put it on the hill and he thought that he had never been so sad. A tearing sadness.

But there was not life in it. There was not life.

And when he got back to the lean-to or thought he did or wished he did she was either asleep or unconscious and he fell back on the skin and slept with her.

And he wished then that he had stayed in his village.

And these things happened when Russel's life folded into the dream and the dream folded into his life:

Nancy lay for five days in the lean-to while Russel fed her meat from the bear, warming small pieces on the end of a willow and handing them to her.

But there was some trouble he did not understand with the woman and soon she went back to being a girl-woman, looking small and pale, and when those five days had passed he knew they would have to go.

"You need help," he said. "From a doctor. We will have to go to a settlement."

She said nothing. Her face had taken on the yellow of the lamp but it was the wrong yellow, the kind of yellow that stayed even when he opened the tent flap and let the daylight in.

"Here is the way it is," he told her, though he was not sure she knew what he meant, or even that she listened. "I do not know for sure where we are or how far we've come. But I think it is closer to the north coast and a village there than it would be to try to get back to your village. We came a long way. My dogs are strong." Even now, he thought, even now it is hard to keep pride away. "So I think we will go to the carcass of the bear and get meat and fat and then run for the north. As before. It should not be far to the edge of the land and there will be a village as there are villages along the coast everywhere and there will be help for you." It was the longest talk he had made since finding her. "That is the way it is."

Still she said nothing. But she nodded so he knew that even weak she understood and had been listening and he felt better for that.

So began the race.

The dogs were strong almost past measuring. Though there were only four left they had been fed meat and run so their legs rippled and were hard to the touch. Their heads were also hard. They had seen and done much and now they knew the man on the sled, knew that he was part of them, knew that no matter what happened he would be there and that made them stronger still. The strength in them came back to Russel and he fed on it and returned it as more strength still.

We have fire, he thought as they left the camp and went for meat to begin the final leg of the run. We have fire between us that grows and grows. Fire that will take us north to safety, fire that will save Nancy.

So began the race.

They took meat from the bear, as much as Russel thought they could carry, but had to leave the hide, the beautiful hide, because it was too heavy. He took the skin from the front legs to make pants, but the rest had to stay.

She brightened when they reached the dead bear. "You did this," she whispered. "With a spear you did this?"

He looked away. "And with the dogs. A man does not kill a bear alone. The dogs helped."

"Still. It is a huge thing, is it not?"

And now he chose not to answer. The dead bear made him sad, doubly so because they had to leave so much behind. It seemed wrong to talk of it as being a big thing—killing the bear with the lance. He did not wish to speak cheaply of it, or brag of it.

So began the race.

They left the bear and headed north again, running in sun and light wind. In the dark and some gentle snow they ran; up the edge of the saucer of light they ran, day into day they ran for six days, stopping only to feed the dogs and rest them in three- and four-hour naps, sleeping on the sled—or Russel sleeping next to it and Nancy on the skins—then up and gone again.

I must win this race, Russel thought. I must win. The girl-woman named Nancy got worse, grew weaker, but his strength grew with her weakness, his strength grew and went into the dogs.

Now they had more light. Winter was still there, but the sun was coming back and he ran through the sun, grateful for the warmth. Even the nights were not so cold.

The dogs did not go down now. They were everything he would have wanted them to be and he drove them with his mind, drove them to the edge of the land, drove them until he felt the land start to tip down and then he smelled it, finally saw the sea ice out ahead.

When he got them to the edge of the sea he stopped and leaned over.

"See? We are north. We have come to the edge of the land."

She was still, but the edges of her eyes were glowing with life, with happiness, with the pride in his voice at what his dogs had done. She was weak, weak and down, but there was still life, enough life, and the corners of her mouth turned up in a smile, a smile that went into Russel.

"See?" he said, raising the team. "We will be in a village soon."

And he brought them up and ran them with his thoughts and on the ice they cut a snowmachine trail and he followed it to the left because that is what his leader said to do and he was the leader and the leader was him.

They drove down the coast, drove on the edge of the sea-ice and land-snow, drove into the soft light of the setting spring sun, drove for the coastal village that had to be soon; the man-boy and the woman-girl and the driving mind-dogs that came from Russel's thoughts and went out and out and came from the dreamfold back.

Back.

Part Three

Dogsong

Part Three

Come, see my dogs.

> *Out before me*
> *they go,*
> *in the long line to the sea.*
> *Out they go.*

Come, see my dogs.

> *They carry me*
> *into all things, all things I will be;*
> *all things that will come to me*
> *will come to my dogs.*
> *I stand on the earth and I sing.*

Come, see my dogs.

> *See them, see them*
> *in the smoke of my life,*
> *in the eyes of my children,*
> *in the sound of my feet,*
> *in the dance of my words.*
> *I stand on the earth and I sing.*

Come, see my dogs.

> *My dogs are what lead me,*
> *they are what move me.*
> *See my dogs in the steam,*
> *in the steam of my life.*
> *They are me.*

Come, see my dogs.

> *I was nothing before them,*
> *no man*
> *and no wife.*
> *Without them, no life,*
> *no girl-woman breathing*
> *no song.*

Come, see my dogs.

   With them I ran,
   ran north to the sea.
   I stand by the sea and I sing.
   I sing of my hunts
   and of Oogruk.

Come, see my dogs.

   Out before me they go.
   Out before me they curve
   in the long line out
   before me
   they go, I go, we go. They are me.

Related Readings

CONTENTS

A Mother's Yarn

It takes a woman's wisdom to survive.

from I Breathe a New Song

selected by Richard Lewis

*Russel urges Oogruk, the Eskimo shaman,
to speak of the old songs, the personal
expressions of individual lives and
struggles. As you read these Copper
Eskimo and Ammassalik Eskimo poems,
think of what Russel would learn from
them.*

Glorious it is to see
The caribou flocking down from the forests
And beginning
Their wanderings to the north.
5   Timidly they watch
For the pitfalls of man.
Glorious it is to see
The great herds from the forests
Spreading out over plains of white.
10 Glorious to see.

Glorious it is to see
Early summer's short-haired caribou
Beginning to wander.
Glorious to see them trot
15 To and fro
Across the promontories,
Seeking a crossing place.

Glorious it is
To see the great musk oxen

20 Gathering in herds.
The little dogs they watch for
When they gather in herds.
Glorious to see.

Glorious it is
25 To see young women
Gathering in litle groups
And paying visits in the houses—
Then all at once the men
Do so want to be manly,
30 While the girls simply
Think of some little lie.

Glorious it is
To see long-haired winter caribou
Returning to the forests.
35 Fearfully they watch
For the little people,
While the herd follows the ebb-mark of the sea
With a storm of clattering hooves.
Glorious it is
40 When wandering time is come.

COPPER ESKIMO

Signal Song on Capture of Polar Bear

I sing for a moment and vaguely
What I, and just today,
Have got the wish to tell of in my poem,
Have got the wish to mention in my song:
5 That on the way northwards, up there northwards
When we went to meet each other,
That on the way northwards, up there northwards,
When we pursued and chased each other from all sides,
In singing my petting songs to get him to sleep,
10 That on the way northwards, up there northwards
   I overtook him and fetched him.

AMMASSALIK ESKIMO

Paddler's Song on Bad Hunting Weather

I got my poem in perfect order.
On the threshold of my tongue
Its arrangement was made.
But I failed, indeed, in my hunting

AMMASSALIK ESKIMO

Who Am I?

by Patty Harjo

Patty Harjo's Native American name is Ya-ka-nes. She is a descendant of the Seminole and Seneca tribes. What does her sense of who she is have in common with Russel's quest?

"Who am I?" This is a question I have asked myself many times.

I am my parents and their parents and all their ancestors before them. I am all the people I have ever met and I am going to be all the people I will ever meet. Also, I am all the forces and objects with which I come in contact. I am the wind, the trees, the birds and the darkness.

I was born of two heritages—both proud, both noble. They clung to their ancient cultures—North and South. Their ancestral roots were transplanted to a new land of adjustment, grief, pain and sorrow, to a future unknown.

Theirs was a future that seemed only a candle in the darkness, a candle of hope for a new beginning. This was a land of disappointment. It was unlike the old. This was a land called Indian Territory and then Oklahoma. In this land all tribes became one, all cultures and heritages began moving onward toward the sun.

Now our sun shines bright, our future is growing clear. We hide our grief, pain and fears. We are moving on. We try to grasp our culture that has slipped away.

We ask, "Who am I?" and our answer comes to us from the distance, "You are all the things you have ever known and will ever know."

Susan Butcher
from Champions

by Bill Littlefield

Both Susan Butcher and Russel measure progress in terms of their close communication with their sled dogs. How else might the views of this top Iditarod competitor mirror Russel's?

For Susan Butcher, it was a day like any other: brutally cold, windy, and snowing hard enough so that it was impossible to see more than a few feet in front of the heavy four-wheel vehicle her sled dogs were dragging for practice. In short, as far as she was concerned, everything was perfect.

Then suddenly Butcher's lead dog went "gee" (right) when Butcher shouted "Haw!" (left), and the four-wheeler, the dogs, and Butcher plunged off a twelve-foot cliff and into a clump of alder trees.

There was, of course, no path out. The trail Butcher and the dogs had fallen from was little traveled, and she figured it might be several days before somebody happened by. She had no saw and no ax. It was only supposed to be a little training run. With pliers, a wrench, and a broken screwdriver, she chopped at the adlers. She got the dogs working together, and they pulled the four-wheeler up the hill. Sometimes, they'd make as little as twelve inches of progress before Butcher would have to begin hacking away with her pliers and wrench again, but five hours after they'd fallen, Butcher and her dogs were on the road back to her cabin. Butcher had learned not to leave home, even for practice, without all her tools. And she hoped her lead dog had learned that "Haw!" meant "Haw!"

On that day when she and her team fell off the trail, Susan Butcher was training herself and her dogs for the Iditarod, the annual sled dog race that covers the eleven hundred miles between Anchorage and Nome, Alaska. Over the years, Butcher's consistently excellent finishes in this most grueling of athletic events have become the stuff of legend, and some of the tales of her training runs are no less dramatic than the races themselves. In a funny way, Butcher's preparation for the Iditarod began before the race ever existed. When she finally entered it for the first time in 1978, Butcher must have felt like she'd finally discovered where she belonged.

As a little girl growing up in Cambridge, Massachusetts, Susan Butcher only knew where she did *not* belong. She hated the congestion of the busy streets, the constant noise of traffic, and the pollution all around her. She begged her parents to move to the country, or at least to let her live in a tent in the backyard. Her best friends were the dogs she kept. In first grade she wrote an essay entitled "I Hate Cities." That was the first, last, and only sentence in the paper.

When she was finally old enough to leave home, she put Cambridge behind her in favor of Colorado. When the Rockies no longer seemed sufficiently remote, she headed for Alaska. She finally settled in a town called Eureka, which you will not find on many maps. There she cobbled together four one-room cabins, a doorless outhouse, and 120 doghouses. Butcher's dogs have outnumbered the two-legged citizens of Eureka by as many as 150 to 13.

Eureka is a fine place to prepare for the Iditarod, since a chief feature of both is isolation. A pitcher who's gone to a full count on the batter with the bases loaded in the ninth inning of a tie game might feel lonely. A marathoner who has run beyond whatever certainty her training can provide and still has miles to go might feel that way, too. But the Iditarod exists primarily as a tribute to the conviction that everybody ought to be able to take care of himself or herself with the help of a dozen or so dogs, and there is perhaps no loneliness like the loneliness of someone lost and snow-blind in the middle of Alaska.

A very fast and disciplined dog team with an experienced and fortunate musher can complete the race in a little over eleven days. Some competitors take as long as three weeks, and a lot of starters, as high as 30 or 40 percent some years, quit. Leaders and losers alike spend hours alone and cold in a blasted white landscape. When their dog teams are traveling up a hill, the mushers run along behind them or kick with first one numb foot, then the other. When the teams are traveling downhill, the mushers hold on for their lives and pray that the wind won't freeze their eyes shut or tear the sled from their hands, leaving them without even the company of their dogs. For as long as they can stand it, they swerve over frozen rivers, navigate through the stumps of burned-over forests by the insanely inadequate glow of a single small headlight, and hope they won't suddenly crash headlong into a bear or a moose or the dog team of some poor fool who has become completely confused and started racing backward on the trail.

All these obstacles appeal to Susan Butcher, who's felt since early childhood that taking heat, light, and shelter for granted was missing the point. Only when she has felt close to nature's essentials has she felt challenged. And only when she has felt challenged has she felt entirely alive.

Joe Redington invented the Iditarod in 1973. He'd always loved the wilderness, particularly the Alaskan wilderness, and he was worried that what he loved was falling into the hands of snowmobilers and settlers with satellite dishes. He scratched his head and wondered how to remind everybody of the toughness and independence that Alaska had always demanded of its residents, and he came up with a race that would require sled drivers and their dogs to brave screaming winds, blinding blizzards, hunger, lack of sleep, and a dozen other hardships that most athletes would just as soon consider only from a great distance. He called the race the Iditarod after ans Alaskan ghost town bearing the name, which is an old Indian word meaning distant place.

Joe Redington first met Susan Butcher a few years after he'd come up with the Iditarod, and right away he was sure she'd win it one day. Or he was almost sure. He proposed a sled dog trek to the summit of Alaska's Denali, also known as Mount McKinley, perhaps partly to test the mettle of this remarkable young woman who'd come to the far north in search of escape from cars, buildings, and too many people. Together with seven dogs and a sled, Butcher and Redington made the 20,320-foot climb through hundred-mile-an-hour winds and over 2,000-foot-deep crevasses. It took them forty-four days. Nobody'd mushed that route before. Nobody's done it since. When they were finished, Redington was *absolutely* sure Susan Butcher would one day win the Iditarod.

But the extent to which Ms. Butcher fulfilled his

prophesy must have surprised even Redington himself. Perhaps it shouldn't have. By the time she began to pile up first-place finishes in the Iditarod and other races in the late eighties, Susan Butcher had paid her dues. She'd learned from her limping pups to line up several friends year-round to help her knit booties for race days. Run out of booties on the trail, and the ice would cut the best team's paws to hamburger. She'd learned how to recognize a potential lead dog in a litter and how to raise all the dogs in her team to have confidence in her. And perhaps most important, she'd learned that her loyalty and attention to the needs of her canine partners would sometimes be rewarded by the special gifts the dogs had to give.

Eight years before she ever won an Iditarod, Butcher was mushing perhaps the best lead dog ever, Tekla, and fourteen other huskies across a frozen river in a practice run when suddenly Tekla began pulling hard to the right. Butcher kept tugging on the team to follow the trail, but Tekla wouldn't respond. Though she'd never balked before, the dog insisted on pulling the sled off the trail to the right. Butcher finally shrugged and decided to follow Tekla's lead. A moment after she'd made that decision and left the track, the whole trail itself sank into the river. "She [Tekla] had a sixth sense that saved our lives," Butcher told Sonja Steptoe of *Sports Illustrated* years later. "That day I learned that the wilderness is their domain. The dogs know more about it than I do, and I'm better off trusting their instincts."

Of course instinct is only part of it. Courage, stamina, and a cool head help, too. In 1985, with a superb team and high expectations, Susan Butcher seemed to be on her way to winning the Iditarod for the first time. But she ran into a problem no measure of preparation or instinct could have forestalled. Veering around a sharp bend in the trail one night, she was startled to find in the beam of her headlight a full-grown female moose. The dog team hit the animal before Butcher knew the moose was there. By the time Butcher could figure out what had happened, the moose was hopelessly entangled in the harnesses that connected the dogs. In the carnage that followed, two of Butcher's dogs were kicked to death and several others were badly injured. While Butcher fought to free the remainign dogs from their harnesses, the moose stomped on her shoulder and might have killed her, too, if another musher hadn't arrived on the scene and shot the moose. Butcher and her team limped to the next checkpoint and resigned from that Iditarod in the low point of her racing career.

And then, beginning in 1986, the high points began coming in quick succession. Between 1986 and 1990, she won the Iditarod four times. The hottest-selling T-shirt in the state bore the legend "Alaska: Where Men Are Men and Women Win the Iditarod." After Butcher's third win in a row in 1988, Joe Redington laughed and told a reporter, "It's getting pretty damn hard for a man to win anything anymore. Maybe we should start a race especially for them."

It has been suggested that the formula for winning the Iditarod involves having good dogs, a good musher, and good luck—in about equal measure. The good musher is the one who can smile into the wrath of an unexpected hundred-mile-per-hour wind, but he or she better make sure the smile is behind several layers of ski mask, because when the wind joins below-zero temperatures, a smile will freeze on the lips for hours, and maybe forever.

Susan Butcher proved she could brave the most vicious weather, but by the time she started winning the Iditarod, she'd learned to prepare herself and her dogs so well that all but the most hideous storms seemed routine. She's also learned that by working closely with her dogs every day from the hour they were born, she could build a level of trust and loyalty that her competitors could only envy. Of course, this relationship demanded a good deal from Butcher, too. In 1991, she passed up the chance to win her fifth Iditarod when she decided that a blizzard raging over the last hundred miles of the course would unreasonably endanger her team. She prolonged a rest stop, waiting for the weather to improve, and finished second that year.

Even when the blizzards hold off and the moose stay out of the way, the Iditarod demands a tremendous amount from a musher. The rules require one mandatory rest period of twenty-four hours during the race, and once having met that requirement, no serious competitor stops for more than four hours at a time. Nearly all of the four hours of each stop are taken up by feeding the dogs, melting the snow so they'll have water, checking their paws for cuts or cracks, mending the harnesses, and maybe catching something to eat—hot chocolate if you're fortunate enough to be stopping at a checkpoint where somebody's cooking, melted snow if you're not.

That doesn't leave much time for sleep, so the Iditarod's exhausted competitors have been known to hallucinate on the trail. In a book entitled *Woodsong*, a musher named Gary Paulsen wrote of a fellow who appeared on his sled wearing horn-rimmed glasses, clutching a stack of important papers. "He is the most boring human being I have ever met," Paulsen says in his diary-like account. "He speaks in a low voice about federal education grants and he goes on and on until at last I yell at him to shut up. The dogs stop and look back at me and of course I am alone."

Though Susan Butcher also might well be susceptible to hallucinations, her dogs probably know her too well to be surprised by anything she could say or do. Certainly she knows them well enough to astonish her friends. "Folks ask how I can call one hundred and fifty of them by name," she says, "but it's natural. They're like children. If you had one hundred and fifty kids, you'd know all their names, wouldn't you?"

Becoming the world's most successful musher and one of the very few sled dog drivers capable of making a living at the sport has never turnd Susan Butcher's head, though it has gone some way toward fulfilling her dream. "I never got into this to make a lot of money," she told an interviewer before winning her fourth Iditarod, in 1990. "But to live just the way you want, to do what you love to do. . . . How could you have any complaints?"

Still, success at the Iditarod *has* changed Susan Butcher, if only a little. Before she became a celebrity, at least by Alaskan standards, she used to go off and live alone for six months or so. No people, no running water, no nothing. Now, in deference to the fact that people want to contact her and because raising and training 150 dogs takes the sort of money only sponsors can provide, she has a phone in her cabin. She has a husband there, too. His name is David Monson, and as a matter of fact the phone was probably his idea. He serves as Susan Butcher's business manager.

Not all the others who tackle the Iditarod have

been as comfortable with Susan Butcher's triumphs in the race as David Monson has been. Rick Swenson, the only person to have won the race as often as Butcher has, tried for some years to get the Iditarod's organizers to adopt a handicapping system that would, in effect, penalize Butcher and other woman racers for weighing less than the men who mush against them. When that didn't work, Swenson took to intimating that Butcher won only because she had a lead dog of supernatural strength and endurance, an unintentional compliment, since Butcher had raised and trained the dog. Butcher herself tends to shrug off the bitterness of the men who resent a woman's success in a sport they'd like to claim as their own. "Yes, I am a woman," she told writer Carolyn Coman in an interview for the book *Body and Soul.* "Yes, it is a victory for me to win the Iditarod. But it isn't amazing that I, a woman, did it. I did it because I am capable, and women are capable."

Being capable may never before have involved such an effort. Butcher has said on several occasions that training for the Iditarod—which involves raising, feeding, running, and training her dogs as well as keeping herself in shape—is an eleven-month proposition. Small wonder that sometimes she thinks about turning her attention exclusively to some of Alaska's shorter races—the three-, four-, or five-hundred mile jaunts. She already knows these races well. She holds the records in most of them, just as she does for the Iditarod. So easing up a little is a pleasant possibility that occupies Susan Butcher sometimes when she thinks about a post-Iditarod future.

Unhappily, there's an unpleasant possibility that concerns her, too. She has adjusted to the modern improvements David Monson has made in their cabin, but other adjustments won't come so easily to the woman who hated the noise and pollution and hustle of Cambridge when she was a little girl. The authorities have begun to improve the roads up Susan Butcher's way, and Butcher has watched "progress" suspiciously. "In ten years we may have ten or fifteen neighbors," she was overheard to say. "If that happens, we'll be gone."

Words on a Page

by Keith Leckie

Lenore, like Russel, finds herself caught between two cultures. Read on to discover how she pursues her dream.

Characters

Lenore Green—an Ojibway teenager
Pete Green—Lenore's father, a fisherman and trapper
Connie Green—Lenore's mother
Sadie Green—Lenore's younger sister
Miss Walker—Lenore's grade ten teacher
The Principal of Lenore's High School
Various Students
Driver
Man

1 INT. CLASSROOM. DAY

It is a sunny fall afternoon in Lenore's grade ten English class. Sunrays through dust particles in the air. There are a dozen classmates, a mixture of white and native, listening as Lenore reads a story she has written.

Lenore. . . . So on that morning before she left, they went by canoe one last time to those favorite places. It was at first light, when the water is a mirror and the trees are still, as if nature is holding her breath.

155

(*A variety of young faces listen, all enthralled with her story. Camera moves slowly, panning across the classroom, holding on different faces.*)

And there was the beaver and the loon and the hawk circling above the treetops. And below the trout and the sturgeon slipped silently through the black water.

(*Camera stops on one Girl, listening intently, then moves again. Camera holds on two Boys slouching close together, almost touching, but their eyes and attention are on Lenore at the front of the class.*)

Creatures as powerful as the great moose, as small as a minnow. She and her father took their place among them.

(*Camera cuts to Miss Walker, the native teacher. She sits to one side of Lenore listening as intently as the rest. She is very impressed. Camera pans and pulls focus to hold finally on Lenore as she finishes the story. She has memorized most of it and hardly has to look at the page. She speaks very well with skilled emphasis and a personal passion for her words.*)

And in this world there was a peace and harmony that she knew no matter how far she traveled, she would never find again. She understood now why her father had brought her here. She felt the morning sun on her face and the gentle rocking of the canoe and smiled because she knew that here would always be her home.

(*Lenore stops speaking, holds the few pages against her chest with both arms and looks at Miss Walker a little anxiously. There is a hushed silence for a moment.*)

Miss Walker (*quietly*). Lenore, that was beautiful!

(*Lenore gives a shy, tentative smile.*)

What did you think, class?

(*The class gives a collective chatter of positive response, then . . .*)

Girl #1. It was real sad.

Boy #1. It reminded me of . . . like around Shadow River.

Girl #2. It was just like a book.

(*There is a silent moment after this pronouncement.* Lenore *looks at the other students trying to suppress her excitement.*)

(*The bell rings signaling the end of class and the students quickly exit the classroom. When the wave of students has passed,* Lenore *is left still standing there.* Miss Walker *puts a hand on her shoulder.*)

Miss Walker. I'm really very impressed, Lenore. Leave your story on my desk. There are some people I'd like to show it to.

(*Miss Walker then exits, leaving* Lenore *alone. She takes a deep breath then allows herself a beaming smile as she hugs her story against herself.*)

2A EXT. STREAM. AFTERNOON

The prow of a cedar canoe cuts through the calm water. Lenore *and her father* Pete, *in the stern, are canoeing their way up a quiet stream. It is late in the afternoon. The shadows are lengthening, and the sunlight retains the shimmering intensity of this time of day as it filters through the autumn foliage.*

Pete. Good here for beaver. Heavy willow growth. Lots of food. (Lenore *notices a beaver swimming. She points.*)

Lenore. Look, Baba.

(*Shot of beaver swimming. He suddenly slaps his tail loudly and dives—stock shot.*)

He's warning his friends about us.

Pete (*seriously*). You know that a long time ago the beaver only had a little skinny tail.

Lenore. Oh yeah?

(Lenore *looks back smiling expectantly. She knows this is the opening to one of her father's crazy stories.*)

Pete (*storytelling tone*). You see, one day Nanabozho was out paddling his big canoe. He's pretty lazy so he decided if he gave the beaver a big paddle tail, he could tie them on the back and they would push his canoe. But once he had given the beaver a paddle tail, the beaver was too quick to catch. So he didn't get a chance to try it.

Lenore (*only half serious*). D'you think it would work?

Pete. Cheemo and I tried it once.

Lenore. Really?

Pete. Sure! Roped a couple 70 pound beavers on the back of this canoe.

Lenore. What happened?

Pete. Well, they chewed a hole in the canoe and we all sank and they got away!

(Lenore *laughs at this image and turns to look back at her father.*)

Lenore. Serves you right.

(Pete *laughs too. They continue paddling slowly, quietly.*)

2B EXT. BEAVER POND. DAY

They canoe near a bubbling beaver dam with more beaver houses visible.

Pete. You said you had a dream to tell.

Lenore. Yes. (*She turns around in the canoe, facing him.*) It's pretty simple, I guess. I'm standing in the woods. There's a raven flying just above my head. It hovers there. It has something to tell me. (*pause, thinking*) It wants to land . . . but it can't. It only hovers there. It never lands.

(Pete *thinks about the dream very seriously for a moment.*)

Pete. Sounds like a good dream. Can't tell you what it means. Maybe it isn't finished with you yet. (Lenore *smiles. Pause*) You know Cheemo had the same dream for five nights in a row. He dreamed he was swimming underwater.

Lenore. Yeah?

Pete. Every night, same thing. Swimming underwater!

Lenore. Yeah?

Pete. On the sixth day, he couldn't stand it anymore. He jumped into the lake! And no more dream.

(*They both laugh again.*)

We'll go upstream to the next pond and . . .

Lenore (*hesitant*). Baba, I . . .

Pete. What?

Lenore (*feeling bad*). I've got all kinds of homework to do. We've got a lot of tests coming up . . .

Pete. Isn't it enough they have you all day at that school?

Lenore. I'm sorry, Baba.

Pete (*Gruffly*). Never mind.

(Pete *quickly backpaddles to turn the canoe around and they head back the way they came.* Lenore *looks unhappy.*)

3 EXT. SCHOOLYARD. DAY

It is lunch break at school. A number of students are sitting around on the grass and walls eating lunch. Some play volleyball nearby. Lenore *is sitting on a bench reading some poetry to a* Classmate. Sadie, *Lenore's sister, is listening in.* Lenore *reads with feeling from the book.*

Lenore.
"Up on the hill against the sky,
A fir tree rocking its lullaby,
Swings, swings,
Its emerald wings,
Swelling the song that my paddle sings."

Classmate #1. That's neat!

Lenore. Yeah. Pauline Johnson. She's a native poet who traveled all around these lakes almost 100 years ago. Musta been hard to get gas for her outboard then, eh? (*They laugh.* Miss Walker *comes up behind them with a letter in her hand. She crouches behind them.*)

Miss Walker (*excited, smiling*). Lenore? I've got some news for you. I sent your story in to the District Writing Competitions. You have been accepted as a finalist!

(*She shows* Lenore *the letter.* Lenore *and* Sadie *read it together.* Lenore *is both excited and disbelieving.*)

Next week you go down to Thunder Bay to read your story to the judges!

(Lenore *and* Sadie *look at each other in amazement.*)

This is wonderful! If you do well there, they could send you to a special high school in the south. Then maybe to study English at university!

Lenore (*mixed emotions*). University!

Miss Walker. Well, let's see how Thunder Bay goes. We just need a letter of permission from your parents and we're all set!

(Lenore *looks at the letter again, confused and excited.* Miss Walker *smiles at her, then leans forward and gives her a little hug.*)

I'm proud of you.

(Miss Walker *gets up and leaves them. Again* Sadie *and* Lenore *look at each other.*)

Sadie. Nice going!

Lenore (*grinning*). Yeah! I can't believe it! (*frowning*) I just wonder what Baba is going to say.

4 INT. KITCHEN (LENORE'S HOME). EVENING

Lenore, Sadie, *their mother* Connie, *and* Pete *are having fish dinner.* Pete *eats his food hungrily.* Lenore *looks up at him once, then again. Then she notices* Sadie *staring at her impatiently.* Lenore *glares at* Sadie *and they both resume eating.*

Pete (*to all*). Good trout, eh? We caught them way

north of Mulligan Bay. Cold and deep.

(*He takes another huge mouthful.*)

Connie. We should have enough in the freezer to last until Christmas.

Pete. The King of France never ate better than this.

(*There is a moment of silence.* Sadie *can wait no longer.*)

Sadie. Baba, Lenore has something to ask you.

(Pete *and* Connie *look up.* Lenore *glares at* Sadie.)

Pete. Uh huh?

Lenore. Well . . . I've been doing some work at school . . .

Pete. Yeah. So?

Lenore. You know . . . like writing.

(Pete *takes another large bite of fish, only vaguely interested.*)

Anyway . . . the new teacher, Miss Walker, said I've been doing real well . . . and there was a story I wrote . . .

Pete. A what?

Lenore (*hesitating*). Well, a story . . . and they, ah . . .

Sadie (*interrupting*). The story won a contest and now she has to go to Thunder Bay to read it and then they'll send her away to university!

(Lenore *"looks daggers" at* Sadie. *Both* Pete *and* Connie *look at* Lenore *in surprise.*)

Lenore. Can't you shut up!

Pete. University!

(Lenore *passes Pete the letter.*)

Lenore. Well, no! It's only if I win, but . . .

(Pete *glances at the letter then pushes it away.*)

Pete. That's crazy! You're only a young girl! You can forget about going to Thunder Bay.

Lenore. But I have to! I'm representing the school!

Pete. They can find someone else.

Lenore. But they want my story!

Pete. Then send the story to Thunder Bay.

Lenore (*approaching tears*). But I want to go!!

Pete. "Want" and "Can" are not always the same thing.

(Pete *goes back to his dinner.*)

Lenore. You never . . . !

(Lenore *is about to continue her argument but her mother is signaling her not to continue along these lines. Lenore stands up and quickly exits the kitchen.*)

5 INT. CLASSROOM. DAY

The classroom is empty except for Lenore *standing at the front and* Miss Walker *sitting at a desk several rows back.* Lenore *is practicing reading her story with a compelling intensity.*

Lenore. She found her father out behind the shed laying the steaming cedar strips across the frame of a new canoe, his strong hands molding the soft wood. "Baba," she said, "Why can't I visit Aunt Doreen for the summer? I'm not a child anymore. I want to ride a subway, Baba! I want to climb to the top of a skyscraper, and see a museum and go to a play. I want to see the world!" But her father turned away and would not look at her.

(Lenore *stops and thinks about her father for a moment.*)

Miss Walker (*quietly*). Yes. Go on.

(*Suddenly all of* Lenore's *momentum is gone. She appears weary.*)

Lenore. Can we stop now?

Miss Walker. Sure. Sure, that's fine. It's coming along really well, Lenore. Parents' Night will be a good rehearsal for the finals.

(*Pause, looking at* Lenore *who appears distracted*)

Is everything alright?

Lenore. Yes, I'm just tired.

Miss Walker. Good. You get a good sleep. I'll see you tomorrow.

(Lenore *gives her a half-hearted smile and leaves the class-room.* Miss Walker *looks after her, wondering if there is anything wrong.*)

6 INT. KITCHEN (LENORE'S HOUSE). DAY

Lenore *comes into the kitchen, tosses down her books and flops down at the table. Her mother is making bannock bread. They are alone. Her mother notices her unhappiness.*

Connie. How was school?

Lenore. Okay. (*pause*) Actually it was lousy. (*sudden anger*) I just don't understand! Why won't he let me go?!

(Connie *stops work and sits down across from her.*)

Connie (*after a moment*). He's afraid of what will happen to you.

Lenore. He wants to trap me!

Connie. It might seem like that, but he believes he's protecting you.

Lenore (*deflated*). What am I going to do, Mom?

Connie. He's stubborn. The harder you push, the more he digs in his heels. (*pause*) D' you remember the story of the Sun and the Wind, how they had a contest to see who could get the coat off a passing man? The Wind blew as hard as he could, but the man held the coat on tightly. When the Sun had his turn, he shone warm and bright and the man just took off his coat.

Lenore. I should be the sun?

(Connie *nods.*)

Connie. Maybe you could read your story to him.

Lenore. I have to read it on Parents' Night. But he'll never come.

Connie. Maybe this time, if you ask, he will.

(Lenore *looks suddenly hopeful.*)

Lenore. You think so?

Connie (*smiling*). Maybe.

(Lenore *smiles happily.*)

7 EXT. WOODS. DAY

A small cedar tree crashes to the ground near the banks of a stream. Pete stands beside the stump, axe in hand. He wipes a sleeve across his sweating forehead, then quickly begins to trim the branches.

With a smaller axe Lenore competently trims the branches of another downed cedar in the foreground. In the background we see a sturdy lean-to, three-quarters completed, large enough to sleep two or three people with provisions—side walls, open front, firepit. Lenore lifts her ten-foot cedar pole, takes it to the structure and fits it in place, resting on the center beam nailed between two trees.

Pete is suddenly beside her and places his pole beside hers which almost completes the superstructure of the roof. He smiles at her.

Pete. Now the tarp, a good layer of cedar boughs and one snowfall will make it warm and dry. Ron and I'll live here a week for trapping. (*looking at her*) What do you think? You want to come?

Lenore. Where?

Pete. Out on the new trapline in November with Ron and me?

Lenore (*excited*). Yeah! (*then subdued*) But I've got school.

(Pete *turns away to adjust the crosspiece.*)

(*hopefully*) But maybe I can get off for a couple of days.

Pete (*not looking at her*). You think about it.

8 EXT. ROCKY STREAM BED. DAY

Lenore *kneels down on a flat rock. Holding her hair back she drinks from the surface of the black, bubbling stream. Camera at stream level. She looks up, satisfied, her face wet. She watches her father who puts his face right down in the water and shakes his head, splashing and blowing bubbles. He looks up at her and they both laugh, water dripping off their faces.*

Pete *cups some water in his hand and brings it to his lips to drink.* Lenore *watches him a moment.*

Lenore. Sometimes I wish I could be a son for you, Baba.

(Pete *looks up at her curiously at this statement out of the blue.*)

Pete. A son?

Lenore. Yes. I know every father wants a son.

(Pete *considers this as he fills a canteen with water.*)

Pete. I would like a son. Maybe someday . . . (*pause*) but the first time I saw you and you smiled at me, I wouldn't have traded you for ten sons!

(Lenore *smiles at this, watching him fill the canteen.*)

Lenore. Baba?

Pete. Hummm?

Lenore. Parents' Night is on Wednesday.

Pete (*distastefully*). Parents' Night?

Lenore. Yeah. I'm going to read something. Be real nice if you were there.

Pete. I don't have anything to say to those teachers.

Lenore. You don't have to say anything.

Pete (*resisting*). And we're fishing next day. We'll be outfitting the boat.

Lenore. Just for a little while? Maybe? (*pause*) Please?

Pete. Okay. I'm not promising but I'll try.

(Lenore *smiles, her eyes sparkling.*)

9 EXT. OPEN SKY (DREAM). DAY

In slow motion against a blue sky background a single bird comes into frame. Shot in slightly slow motion. It hovers above the camera. After a moment it is joined by other birds . . . two, three, four, all hover in frame above the camera. It is not a threatening image. The motion is beautiful to watch. The sound of wings becomes steadily louder.

10A INT. LENORE'S BEDROOM. NIGHT

Lenore, *with a little gasp, suddenly sits up in bed, staring out in front of her. Her tense body relaxes. She thinks for a moment about the images of the dream. She lies down again and rolls over, her face toward camera. She smiles with excitement and anticipation.*

10B EXT. SPIRIT BAY DOCKS. LATE DAY

A pick-up truck stops beside the docks. Pete *is waiting. The* Driver *gets out and opens the tailgate.*

Driver. Got your new nets, Pete.

(Pete *inspects the three bundles of nets as the* Driver *drops them to the ground.*)

Pete. Hey, they don't have floats!

(*The* Driver *hands him the bill.*)

Driver. See? Nothing about floats.

(Pete *looks at the bill. The* Driver *looks at him, then turns the bill right side up for him to read.* Pete *glances at it and stuffs it into his pocket.*)

Pete. Gonna take me all night to sew floats on these nets.

Driver. You want 'em or not?

(Pete *nods. The* Driver *drops the last net on the ground, gets back in the truck and drives off. As the truck drives away,* Pete *checks his watch, looks unhappy, then carries the first bundle toward the boat.*)

11 INT. SCHOOL AUDITORIUM. EVENING

It's Parents' Night in the small auditorium. There are about two dozen parents present, native and white. Tables display artwork of various kinds and highly graded tests and essays. There is a coffee and pastry table where parents stand in small groups talking with four or five teachers.

There is a podium at the front of the auditorium. Lenore *stands near it anxiously watching the doorway, holding the pages of her story.*

Sadie. Betcha he doesn't come.

Lenore. He'll come.

(Miss Walker *approaches them.*)

Miss Walker. Hi Lenore. Are you ready?

Lenore (*anxious*). I think so.

Miss Walker. You'll do great! Are your parents here yet? I was looking forward to meeting them.

Lenore (*eyeing the doorway*). They'll be here any minute.

(The Principal *moves behind the podium to address those present. Conversation dwindles.*)

Principal. Good evening, and welcome to the first Parents' Night of the year at Nipigon District Junior High School. Glad you could come out. In a moment I'll ask one of our students to come up and read a prize-winning story she's written . . .

(Principal*'s talk continues over dialogue between* Lenore *and* Miss Walker, *below.*)

But first I would like to say a few words about the challenges facing us in the coming year. Never before has there been such an abundance of information and communication in our world . . .

(Lenore *whispers anxiously to* Miss Walker.)

Lenore. Wait! I can't do it yet!

Miss Walker. Don't worry. I'll stall him if necessary. (*smiling*) Mr. Crankhurst goes on forever, anyway.

(Lenore *tries to smile. She looks at the* Principal.)

Principal. It is almost overwhelming when you consider it. In the face of this, a sound education has never been more important. And so, our goal will remain a high standard of academic achievement and individual excellence in all our endeavors. We are deeply aware of our responsibility here at Beardmore to mold the bright minds of young men and women who will in a few short years forge the destiny of our world!

(Connie *comes through the door into the auditorium. She is alone.* Lenore *watches her.* Connie *stops, looks around the room and sees* Lenore. *She looks at her and shakes her head sadly.* Pete *is not coming.* Lenore *appears as if she's about to cry.* Sadie *takes this all in.)*

So now let me introduce one of those bright young minds, to read her story that has been selected for the finals of the District Writing Competition . . . Lenore Green.

(There is polite applause. Lenore *turns to* Miss Walker *in anger and frustration.)*

Lenore. I'm not going to do it.

Miss Walker *(sudden alarm).* What!?

Lenore. Why bother!

(The applause dies out. The Principal *and all others are looking expectantly at* Lenore. *With story in hand,* Lenore *turns and exits the auditorium. There are whispered comments in the audience of parents.* Miss Walker *quickly follows* Lenore.)

12 INT. HALLWAY (SCHOOL). EVENING

The hallway is deserted. Lenore *walks determinedly away from the auditorium.* Miss Walker *comes out the door and calls after her.*

Miss Walker. Lenore! Lenore!

*(Lenore *stops and turns back.* Miss Walker *comes up to her.)*

Miss Walker. What's wrong!? I don't understand.

Lenore. I don't want to read my story. And I don't want to go to Thunder Bay!

Miss Walker. But Lenore! This is a great opportunity! This is the first big step in your career.

Lenore. What career?!

Miss Walker. You could do anything—go to university, become a journalist or an English professor or a playwright. You've been given a talent. You can't turn your back on it!

Lenore. It's only a stupid story. I'm sorry I even wrote it.

(Lenore *throws the story down on the floor, turns and walks away. After a beat* Miss Walker *reaches down and picks up the spilled pages. She looks at them, then watches* Lenore *walking away from her.*)

13A INT. CLASSROOM. MORNING

Miss Walker *is sitting at her desk marking tests in the empty classroom. She works quickly for a moment, but then her momentum slows, her eyes leave her work, and brows knitted she begins to think again about* Lenore. *She can't figure it out.*

Sadie *and* Connie *enter the room behind her.* Connie *is intimidated by a woman of her own generation with a university education. She looks uncomfortably around the room.*

Sadie. Miss Walker?

Miss Walker (*turns around and stands*). Hi Sadie . . . and Mrs. Green. How are you?

(Connie *nods shyly. It takes a moment to find the words, but she speaks them with determination.*)

Connie There is something you should know. Lenore loves to write more than anything. And she wants to go to Thunder Bay. But my husband . . . (*a little ashamed*) he won't let her.

Sadie. Baba doesn't believe in schools and books and stuff.

Miss Walker (*reflectively*). I see. Please sit.

(Miss Walker *gestures to a chair for* Connie *and another for* Sadie.)

13B EXT. SPIRIT BAY DOCKS. AFTERNOON

Pete *is unloading his catch after a good day's fishing. He is on the dock. A* Crewman *hands him a tub full of ice and fish from the deck on the boat. There are several tubs on the dock.*

Pete (*feigning pain*). Uhhh! The only trouble with a good catch is it's bad for my back!

(*The* Crewman *laughs.* Pete *lifts the tub of fish and walks a few steps to the other tubs when he notices* Lenore. Lenore *stands—with school books—at the far end of the dock watching* Pete *from a distance. Other students pass by behind her on their way home.* Lenore *and* Pete *look at each other a moment.* Pete *puts the tub down with the others and wiping his hands with a rag takes a step toward her.* Lenore *turns and quickly walks away.* Pete *stops and watches her, feeling bad.*)

14 INT. CLASSROOM. AFTERNOON

Connie *and* Sadie *are talking to* Miss Walker. Connie *is more relaxed now. She is reflective.*

Connie. When I was Lenore's age, I was real good at school too. Top of my class. I might have gone on to university, even! But I couldn't decide . . . and then I met Pete . . . (*pause, then with conviction*) I want this for Lenore!

Miss Walker. So do I.

Connie. We're having a roast Sunday. Why don't you come by?

(Connie *and* Miss Walker *and* Sadie *share a conspiratorial smile.*)

Miss Walker. Good! I will.

15 EXT. LENORE'S HOUSE. DAY

Establishing shot/time passage. A car and a pickup truck are parked outside.

16 INT. KITCHEN (LENORE'S HOUSE). DAY

The table is nicely laid out with flowers and a bright, plastic tablecloth and a variety of food—fish, slices of moose, potatoes and other vegetables, and bannock bread. Miss Walker *sits at one end of the table,* Pete *at the other.* Sadie *and* Connie *sit on one side,* Lenore *on the other.*

Lenore *is very quiet. She is angry at her father and embarrassed by* Miss Walker *being there. She is uncomfortable to be at the table with both of them.*

Miss Walker *takes a platter of meat from* Lenore.

Miss Walker. Thanks Lenore.

(Pete *is eating his food hungrily, eyes on his plate.* Miss Walker *is talking mostly to* Connie, *although she watches* Pete *for any response.*)

. . . and we're getting in a new portable classroom and adding to the library . . .

(Pete *without looking up grunts his disfavor over this.*)

And what I'm hoping for by the end of the year is a computer terminal for the students to use . . .

Pete (*grunts again*). Pass the moose.

(Miss Walker *finds the platter of moose beside her and passes it. Pete piles moose meat on his plate. Miss Walker looks at him, is about to say something to him, then thinks better of it.*)

Miss Walker. One thing I'm excited about (*She looks at Pete.*) . . . and Mr. Crankhurst seems open to it . . . is an Ojibway Studies course.

(Pete *looks up at this.*)

Pete (*with disdain*). Ojibway Studies?

Miss Walker. Yes. The language and customs and history . . .

Pete. Like one of them dead civilizations in a museum.

Miss Walker. No! Not at all. In fact, you trap and fish. Maybe you'd come in and give demonstrations of your expertise?

Pete. Expertise! If you get paid by the word, that's a ten dollar one for sure!

(Sadie *giggles at this.* Miss Walker *is angry. The gloves are off.*)

Miss Walker. I can see you don't think much of education, but it can give all kinds of things to a girl like Lenore.

Pete. You mean like a one-way ticket out of here.

(Miss Walker *takes out the folded pages of* Lenore*'s story and unfolds them.*)

Miss Walker. Have you read this?

Pete. No.

(Connie *looks worried.*)

Miss Walker. Well I think you should read it!

Pete (*suddenly awkward*). I will . . . later.

Miss Walker. Read it now! Just the first page.

(*She stands up, reaches over and puts the manuscript down in front of him.* Pete *moves it away.* Miss Walker *stays standing.*)

Pete. No.

Miss Walker. Well if you don't care enough to even read . . .

(Pete *stands up angrily.*)

Pete. You saying I don't care about my daughter?!

Miss Walker. She has talent and imagination and desire! You can't imprison her here!

Pete. Prison!

Miss Walker. There's a whole world waiting for her out there!

(Lenore *sits there becoming angry and frustrated listening to this.*)

Pete. In that world she'll be an outsider! She'll be alone and unhappy and forget who she is!

(Lenore *stands up and looks at* Pete.)

Lenore. You don't know who I am! (*then at* Miss Walker) Neither of you! No one even cares what *I* want!

(Lenore *turns away and exits the house.* Pete *and* Miss Walker *look at each other, now sorry that they have been so insensitive.*)

17 EXT. END OF DOCK (SUNSET LODGE). DAY

Lenore crouches on the end of the dock. She looks down at her reflection in the black water. She holds out a pebble and lets it drop into the reflection. When it clears a moment later, her father's reflection can be seen behind. He stands there a moment.

Lenore (*residual anger*). Why won't you read my story?

(*Pete crouches down beside her and looks out at the water a moment. He doesn't look at her as he speaks.*)

Pete. Because . . . I can't.

(*Lenore looks at him in surprise.*)

I never learned to read so good. You never knew, eh?

(*Lenore shakes her head; pause, then bitterly*)

When I went to school there was a teacher . . . If I didn't learn my lessons or talked Indian, he'd beat me with a switch and call me names. One day I took the switch away from him and never went back. Never been in school since.

(*Lenore watches her father, her expression softening.*)

Lenore. Come for a walk?

(*Pete looks up at her for the first time, smiles and nods.*)

18A EXT. SPIRIT BAY FIELD. DAY

A telephoto lens shows Pete and Lenore walking side by side toward camera. The background shows the picturesque village of Spirit Bay on the edge of the lake. They walk in silence for a moment.

Pete. I'm afraid. (*pause*) Afraid that you'll go away and become a stranger to us.

Lenore. How could I do that?!

Pete. If you go south to school. It's very different there.

18B EXT. SPIRIT BAY ROAD. DAY

Pete *and* Lenore *walk toward camera, telephoto lens.*

Lenore. I'll always be Nishnabe, Baba. And Spirit Bay is my home.

Pete. Others have said that and not come back.

Lenore. I'll come back! I want to learn to write better so I can live here and tell about our people! That's why I want to write!

(Pete *thinks about this hard as they walk along. They fall silent again.*)

19 EXT. DREAMER'S ROCK. AFTERNOON

Pete *and* Lenore *sit atop Dreamer's Rock facing the lake that stretches out before them to the horizon. The village can be seen below, and distant islands in the lake.*

Lenore. I've been waiting to tell you the last of the dreams. The dreams of the bird that wants to land.

Pete (*very interested*). Yes! Is it finished?

Lenore. It's finished.

Pete. How did it end?

Lenore. Remember I told you the bird was hovering and trying to land? (Pete *nods.*) Well then each night there were more birds—a few and then dozens . . . then hundreds of birds! (*pause, remembering*) And there was a wide open field of snow! And there they began to land, black against the white snow.

(Pete *is listening intently.*)

Pete. They all landed?

Lenore. Yes! And as each bird landed it became a letter. And the snow was like a page. And the bird-letters formed words. And the words sentences. (*looking at him*) They were my words, Baba! They were the words I wrote!

(Lenore *stops, thinking about the images.* Pete *smiles at her, excited by the dream, but saddened by its meaning.*)

Pete. Sounds like you were meant to be a writer. I won't stop you.

(Lenore *is not satisfied.*)

Lenore. But I need more, Baba. I don't know if I can do it alone. I need your help.

Pete. *My* help? I can't even read!

Lenore. Not that kind. I need your . . . (*pause, finding right word*) courage. Will you come to Thunder Bay and hear me read my story?

Pete (*unhappily*). At the university?

(Lenore *nods.* Pete *hesitates, then answers.*)

I'll come.

(Lenore *takes his hand and smiles at him happily.*)

20A EXT. LAKEHEAD UNIVERSITY. DAY

Establishing shot of university with an identifying sign.

20B INT. UNIVERSITY. DAY

Pete, Lenore, Sadie, Connie *and* Miss Walker *approach a* Man *in a suit outside the lecture room doors.* Pete *looks around uncomfortably.*

Miss Walker (*to* Man). Is this the District Writing Finals?

Man #1 (*officious*). Yes. They're about to begin.

(Lenore *is excited and scared. She hesitates at the door.*)

Lenore. I . . . I don't think . . .

(Pete *puts a hand on her shoulder. She looks up at him.*)

Pete (*smiling*). Read it to me. Just to me.

(Lenore *takes heart in these instructions. She smiles and goes quickly inside followed by the others.*)

21 LECTURE HALL. DAY

The lecture hall is quite full of people. A panel of six judges sits at a table at the front listening as Lenore *reads her story.*

Lenore. So on that morning before she left, they went by canoe one last time to those favorite places. It was at first light, when the water is a mirror and the trees are still, as if nature is holding her breath.

(Near the front rows sit Miss Walker, Pete, Connie *and* Sadie *listening.* Lenore *reads directly to her father inspired by his presence.* Pete *listens intently.*)

And there was the beaver and the loon and the

hawk circling above the treetops. And below, the trout and the sturgeon slipped silently through the black water.

Creatures as powerful as the great moose, as small as the minnow. She and her father took their place among them.

(Pete, *in his solemn features, reveals amazement at his daughter's ability and the touching sentiments of the story.*)

And in this world there was a peace and harmony that she knew no matter how far she traveled, she would never find again.

She understood now why her father had brought her here. She felt the morning sun on her face and the gentle rocking of the canoe and smiled because she knew that here would always be her home.

(*When* Lenore *finishes, the hall is silent.* Pete, *very moved by his daughter's story, rises immediately to his feet. He begins to applaud loudly—the only one in the hall. The* Judges *look at him with disfavor. But then* Sadie *applauds and stands and* Connie *and* Miss Walker *stand applauding and then others and finally the whole hall is on its feet applauding. Even two of the* Judges *give polite applause.* Connie, Miss Walker *and* Sadie *smile at* Pete. Pete *looks only at* Lenore.)

(Pete *and* Lenore, *with tears in her eyes, look at each other and smile meaningfully at one another.*)

The King of Mazy May

by Jack London

*About Russel's quest, Oogruk comments,
"It isn't the destination that counts. It is
the journey." For Walt, who races across
the Yukon Territory with claim jumpers in
hot pursuit, the goal is quite the opposite.*

Walt Masters is not a very large boy, but there is manliness in his make-up, and he himself, although he does not know a great deal that most boys know, knows much that other boys do not know. He has never seen a train of cars nor an elevator in his life, and for that matter he has never once looked upon a cornfield, a plow, a cow, or even a chicken. He has never had a pair of shoes on his feet, nor gone to a picnic or party, nor talked to a girl. But he has seen the sun at midnight, watched the ice jams on one of the mightiest of rivers, and played beneath the northern lights, the one white child in thousands of square miles of frozen wilderness.

Walt has walked all the fourteen years of his life in suntanned, moose-hide moccasins, and he can go to the Indian camps and "talk big" with the men, and trade calico and beads with them for their precious furs. He can make bread without baking powder, yeast, or hops, shoot a moose at three hundred yards, and drive the wild wolf dogs fifty miles a day on the packed trail.

Last of all, he has a good heart, and is not afraid of the darkness and loneliness, of man or beast or thing. His father is a good man, strong and brave, and Walt is growing up like him.

Walt was born a thousand miles or so down the Yukon, in a trading post below the Ramparts. After his mother died, his father and he came up on the river, step by step, from camp to camp, till now they are settled down on the Mazy May Creek in the Klondike country. Last year they and several others had spent much toil and time on the Mazy May, and endured great hardships; the creek, in turn, was just beginning to show up its richness and to reward them for their heavy labor. But with the news of their discoveries, strange men began to come and go through the short days and long nights, and many unjust things they did to the men who had worked so long upon the creek.

Si Hartman had gone away on a moose hunt, to return and find new stakes driven and his claim jumped. George Lukens and his brother had lost their claims in a like manner, having delayed too long on the way to Dawson to record them. In short, it was the old story, and quite a number of the earnest, industrious prospectors had suffered similar losses.

But Walt Masters's father had recorded his claim at the start, so Walt had nothing to fear now that his father had gone on a short trip up the White River prospecting for quartz. Walt was well able to stay by himself in the cabin, cook his three meals a day, and look after things. Not only did he look after his father's claim, but he had agreed to keep an eye on the adjoining one of Loren Hall, who had started for Dawson to record it.

Loren Hall was an old man, and he had no dogs, so he had to travel very slowly. After he had been gone some time, word came up the river that he had broken through the ice at Rosebud Creek and frozen his feet so badly that he would not be able to travel for a couple of weeks. Then Walt Masters received the news that old Loren was nearly all right again, and about to move on afoot for Dawson as fast as a weakened man could.

Walt was worried, however; the claim was liable to be jumped at any moment because of the delay, and a fresh stampede had started in on Mazy May. He did not like the looks of the newcomers, and one day, when five of them came by with crack dog teams and the lightest of camping outfits, he could see they were prepared to make speed, and resolved to keep an eye on them. So he locked up the cabin and followed them, being at the same time careful to remain hidden.

He had not watched them long before he was sure that they were professional stampeders, bent on jumping all the claims in sight. Walt crept along the snow at the rim of the creek and saw them change many stakes, destroy old ones, and set up new ones.

In the afternoon, with Walt always trailing on their heels, they came back down the creek, unharnessed their dogs, and went into camp within two claims of his cabin. When he saw them make preparations to cook, he hurried home to get something to eat himself, and then hurried back. He crept so close that he could hear them talking quite plainly, and by pushing the underbrush aside he could catch occasional glimpses of them. They had finished eating and were smoking around the fire.

"The creek is all right, boys," a large, black-bearded man, evidently the leader, said, "and I think the best thing we can do is to pull out tonight. The dogs can follow the trail: besides, it's going to be moonlight. What say you?"

"But it's going to be beastly cold," objected one of the party. "It's forty below zero now."

"An' sure, can't ye keep warm by jumpin' off the sleds an' runnin' after the dogs?" cried an Irishman. "An' who wouldn't? The creek's as rich as a United States mint! Faith, it's an ilegant chanst to be gettin' a run fer yer money! An' if ye don't run, it's mebbe you'll not get the money at all, at all."

"That's it," said the leader. "If we can get to Dawson and record, we're rich men; and there's no telling who's been sneaking along in our tracks, watching us, and perhaps now off to give the alarm. The thing for us to do is to rest the dogs a bit, and then hit the trail as hard as we can. What do you say?"

Evidently the men had agreed with their leader, for Walt Masters could hear nothing but the rattle of the tin dishes which were being washed. Peering out cautiously, he could see the leader studying a piece of paper. Walt knew what it was at a glance—a list of all the unrecorded claims on Mazy May. Any man could get these lists by applying to the gold commissioner at Dawson.

"Thirty-two," the leader said, lifting his face to the men. "Thirty-two isn't recorded, and this is thirty-three. Come on: let's take a look at it. I saw somebody had been working on it when we came up this morning."

Three of the men went with him, leaving one to remain in camp. Walt crept carefully after them till they came to Loren Hall's shaft. One of the men went down and built a fire on the bottom to thaw out the frozen gravel, while the others built another fire on the dump and melted water in a couple of gold pans. This they poured into a piece of canvas stretched between two logs, used by Loren Hall in which to wash his gold.

In a short time a couple of buckets of dirt were sent up by the man in the shaft, and Walt could see the others grouped anxiously about their leader as he proceeded to wash it. When this was finished, they stared at the broad streak of black sand and yellow gold grains on the bottom of the pan, and one of them called excitedly for the man who had remained in camp to come. Loren Hall had struck it rich and his claim was not yet recorded. It was plain that they were going to jump it.

Walt lay in the snow, thinking rapidly. He was only a boy, but in the face of the threatened injustice to old lame Loren Hall he felt that he must do something. He waited and watched, with his mind made up, till he saw the men begin to square up new stakes. Then he crawled away till out of hearing, and broke into a run for the camp of the stampeders. Walt's father had taken their own dogs with him prospecting, and the boy knew how impossible it was for him to undertake the seventy miles to Dawson without the aid of the dogs.

Gaining the camp, he picked out, with an experienced eye, the easiest running sled and started to harness up the stampeders' dogs. There were three teams of six each, and from these he chose ten of the best. Realizing how necessary it was to have a good head dog, he strove to discover a leader amongst them; but he had little time in which to do it, for he could hear the voices of the returning men. By the time the team was in shape and everything ready, the claim-jumpers came into sight in an open place not more than a hundred yards from the trail, which ran down the bed of the creek. They cried out to Walt, but instead of giving heed to them he grabbed up one of their fur sleeping robes, which lay loosely in the snow, and leaped upon the sled.

"Mush! Hi! Mush on!" he cried to the animals, snapping the keen-lashed whip among them.

The dogs sprang against the yoke straps, and the sled jerked under way so suddenly as to almost throw him off. Then it curved into the creek, poising perilously on the runner. He was almost breathless with suspense, when it finally righted with a bound and sprang ahead again. The creek bank was high and he could not see the men, although he could hear their cries and knew they were running to cut him off. He did not dare to think what would happen if they caught him; he just clung to the sled, his heart beating wildly, and watched the snow rim of the bank above him.

Suddenly, over this snow rim came the flying body of the Irishman, who had leaped straight for the sled in a desperate attempt to capture it; but he was an instant too late. Striking on the very rear of it, he was thrown from his feet, backward, into the snow. Yet, with the quickness of a cat, he had clutched the end of the sled with one hand, turned over, and was dragging behind on his breast, swearing at the boy and threatening all kinds of terrible things if he did not stop the dogs; but Walt cracked him sharply across the knuckles with the butt of the dog whip until he let go.

It was eight miles from Walt's claim to the Yukon—eight very crooked miles, for the creek wound back and forth like a snake, "tying knots in itself," as George Lukens said. And because it was so crooked the dogs could not get up their best speed, while the sled ground heavily on its side against the curves, now to the right, now to the left.

Travelers who had come up and down the Mazy

May on foot, with packs on their backs, had declined to go round all the bends, but instead had made shortcuts across the narrow necks of the creek bottom. Two of his pursuers had gone back to harness the remaining dogs, but the others took advantage of these shortcuts, running on foot, and before he knew it they had almost overtaken him.

"Halt!" they cried after him. "Stop, or we'll shoot!"

But Walt only yelled the harder at the dogs, and dashed around the bend with a couple of revolver bullets singing after him. At the next bend they had drawn up closer still, and the bullets struck uncomfortably near him but at this point the Mazy May straightened out and ran for half a mile as the crow flies. Here the dogs stretched out in their long wolf swing, and the stampeders, quickly winded, slowed down and waited for their own sled to come up.

Looking over his shoulder, Walt reasoned that they had not given up the chase for good, and that they would soon be after him again. So he wrapped the fur robe about him to shut out the stinging air, and lay flat on the empty sled, encouraging the dogs, as he well knew how.

At last, twisting abruptly between two river islands, he came upon the mighty Yukon sweeping grandly to the north. He could not see from bank to bank, and in the quick-falling twilight it loomed a great white sea of frozen stillness. There was not a sound, save the breathing of the dogs, and the churn of the steel-shod sled.

No snow had fallen for several weeks, and the traffic had packed the main river trail till it was hard and glassy as glare ice. Over this the sled flew along, and the dogs kept the trail fairly well, although Walt quickly discovered that he had made a mistake in choosing the leader. As they were driving in single file, without reins, he had to guide them by his voice, and it was evident the head dog had never learned the meaning of "gee" and "haw." He hugged the inside of the curves too closely, often forcing his comrades behind him into the soft snow, while several times he thus capsized the sled.

There was no wind, but the speed at which he traveled created a bitter blast, and with the thermometer down to forty below, this bit through fur and flesh to the very bones. Aware that if he remained constantly upon the sled he would freeze to death, and knowing the practice of Arctic travelers, Walt shortened up one of the lashing thongs, and whenever he felt chilled, seized hold of it, jumped off, and ran behind till warmth was restored. Then he would climb on and rest till the process had to be repeated.

Looking back he could see the sled of his pursuers, drawn by eight dogs, rising and falling over the ice hummocks like a boat in a seaway. The Irishman and the black-bearded leader were with it, taking turns in running and riding.

Night fell, and in the blackness of the first hour or so Walt toiled desperately with his dogs. On account of the poor lead dog, they were continually floundering off the beaten track into the soft snow, and the sled was as often riding on its side or top as it was in the proper way. This work and strain tried his strength sorely. Had he not been in such haste he could have avoided much of it, but he feared the stampeders would creep up in the darkness and overtake him. However, he could hear them yelling to their dogs, and knew from the sounds they were coming up very slowly.

When the moon rose he was off Sixty Mile, and Dawson was only fifty miles away. He was almost exhausted, and breathed a sigh of relief as he climbed on the sled again. Looking back, he saw his enemies had crawled up within four hundred yards. At this space they remained, a black speck of motion on the white river breast. Strive as they could, they could not shorten this distance, and strive as he would, he could not increase it.

Walt had now discovered the proper lead dog, and he knew he could easily run away from them if he could only change the bad leader for the good one. But this was impossible, for a moment's delay, at the speed they were running, would bring the men behind upon him.

When he was off the mouth of Rosebud Creek, just as he was topping a rise, the report of a gun and the ping of a bullet on the ice beside him told him that they were this time shooting at him with a rifle. And from then on, as he cleared the summit of each ice jam, he stretched flat on the leaping sled till the rifle shot from the rear warned him that he was safe till the next ice jam was reached.

Now it is very hard to lie on a moving sled, jumping and plunging and yawing like a boat before the wind, and to shoot through the deceiving moonlight at an object four hundred yards away on another moving sled performing equally wild antics. So it is not to be wondered at that the black-bearded leader did not hit him.

After several hours of this, during which, perhaps, a score of bullets had struck about him, their ammunition began to give out and their fire slackened. They took greater care, and shot at him at the most favorable opportunities. He was also leaving them behind, the distance slowly increasing to six hundred yards.

Lifting clear on the crest of a great jam off Indian River, Walt Masters met with his first accident. A bullet sang past his ears, and struck the bad lead dog.

The poor brute plunged in a heap, with the rest of the team on top of him.

Like a flash Walt was by the leader. Cutting the traces with his hunting knife, he dragged the dying animal to one side and straightened out the team.

He glanced back. The other sled was coming up like an express train. With half the dogs still over their traces, he cried "Mush on!" and leaped upon the sled just as the pursuers dashed abreast of him.

The Irishman was preparing to spring for him—they were so sure they had him that they did not shoot—when Walt turned fiercely upon them with his whip.

He struck at their faces, and men must save their faces with their hands. So there was no shooting just then. Before they could recover from the hot rain of blows, Walt reached out from his sled, catching their wheel dog by the forelegs in midspring and throwing him heavily. This snarled the team, capsizing the sled and tangling his enemies up beautifully.

Away Walt flew, the runners of his sled fairly screaming as they bounded over the frozen surface. And what had seemed an accident proved to be a blessing in disguise. The proper lead dog was now to the fore, and he stretched low and whined with joy as he jerked his comrades along.

By the time he reached Ainslie's Creek, seventeen miles from Dawson, Walt had left his pursuers, a tiny speck, far behind. At Monte Cristo Island he could no longer see them. And at Swede Creek, just as daylight was silvering the pines, he ran plump into the camp of Loren Hall.

Almost as quick as it takes to tell it, Loren had his sleeping furs rolled up, and had joined Walt on the sled. They permitted the dogs to travel more slowly, as there was no sign of the chase in the rear, and just as they pulled up at the gold commissioner's office in Dawson, Walt, who had kept his eyes open to the last, fell asleep.

And because of what Walt Masters did on this night, the men of the Yukon have become proud of him, and speak of him now as the King of Mazy May.

The First Americans

by Marion Wood

*Oogruk passes on what he knows about
the old ways to someone from a younger
generation. See what common elements
you can recognize between Oogruk's way
of life and the lives of North America's first
inhabitants.*

Archaeologists believe that the first inhabitants of
America were bands of hunters who crossed the
Bering Strait from Siberia about 25,000 years ago.
Then much of the continent was covered with ice,
but, as this began to melt, people gradually moved
south until, about 10,000 years ago, they reached the
very tip of South America.

With the passing of the last Ice Age, North
America developed into a land of immense variety
and contrast. Extending from the Arctic wastes of
northern Canada and Alaska to the sub-tropical
regions of Florida and California, it is a land of high
mountain ranges and dense forests, fertile river
valleys and wide grassy plains, swamps and deserts.
The Indians of North America followed different
ways of life according to the type of region which
they inhabited, developing skills and traditions best
suited to the natural environment and the resources
which it offered.

In the far north, around the Arctic coasts, lived the
Eskimos, nomadic hunters who depended on both
land and sea for their livelihood. Seals, walrus,
whales and caribou provided them not only with

food, but also with blubber and fat for heat and light and skins for clothing, shelter and boats. In winter seals and walrus were hunted through holes cut in the ice, but in summer, when the ice broke up, they were harpooned from light canoes called kayaks. Whales were hunted from larger open boats, or umiaks, which could carry eight or ten men.

Eskimo clothing provided extremely good protection against the harsh climate. Sealskin was used for summer clothing, but warmer caribou hide was preferred for winter. Both men and women wore hooded parkas with trousers, boots and mittens, often two layers of each in very cold weather.

During the summer months people lived in skin tents, but in winter they built more permanent dwellings of stone, wood and turf. Where these materials were not available, domed snowhouses, or igloos, were constructed from blocks of hard-packed snow and ice. Several families usually lived together in one large house or in a cluster of igloos linked by a common entrance tunnel. Often, settlements consisted of only one or two such family groups, except when several groups came together for communal hunting or for religious ceremonies.

The coastal areas inhabited by the Eskimos were almost completely treeless, but further south stretched great forests of pine, spruce, larch and cedar. The Indians who lived here were few in number and widely scattered. They were also hunters and fishermen, travelling in small groups during the long, dark winter months and coming together in small camps for the short summer.

Like the Eskimos, the Indians of the Northern Forests needed to consume large quantities of food to combat the cold and to gain energy for hunting. Caribou, moose, bears, beavers and hares were trapped or hunted with bows and arrows. Birds were caught in nets and snares, and around the lakes, fishing was important, especially at times of the year when other forms of food were scarce.

The most common shelter was a conical tent of skin or bark, which was easily constructed and transported, although in the western part of the area more substantial wood houses were built.

Caribou and moose skins were used for making clothing and bedding, as well as bags for carrying goods and belongings. Other storage containers and dishes for cooking and serving were made from pieces of birch bark, folded into shape and then stitched with spruce roots.

Birch bark was also used for making canoes. Large sheets were fastened to a wooden framework, again with spruce roots, and the seams coated with spruce gum to make them watertight. Birchbark canoes were very light and could be easily carried around rapids or between one waterway and another.

In winter, sleds and toboggans were used for hauling goods, and snowshoes were worn, designed to prevent the wearer from sinking into the snow.

Just as the lives of North American Indians differed from one area to another, so did their beliefs and myths, for these reflected their experience of the world. The hunting tribes, for example, told many stories of animal spirits, while those who were farmers were more concerned with beings who, they believed, controlled rainfall and growth of crops.

All these spirits had to be treated with respect and caution, for, although they could be called upon for help in time of need, they could also be dangerous and there were many complicated rules of conduct to be followed if the spirits were not to be angered and cause storms, sickness, famine and other calamities to strike mankind. Hunters, for example, often treated the animals which they killed with great ceremony so that their spirits might be placated and return to be hunted again. Those who broke the rules and offended the spirits could bring hardship and suffering not only to themselves, but to the whole community. Many of the Indian myths explain the origin of these rules and how they should be followed.

Other stories tell of individuals receiving the help of spirits through personal contact with them. Young men wishing to make their way in the world often sought such help by going alone into remote and desolate places to fast and pray for guidance After denying themselves food and water for several days, they often had visions in which spirits appeared to befriend them and to instruct them in rituals which would bring them wealth and success.

A man who was blessed with special help from the spirits could become a medicine man, or shaman, and use the knowledge for good or harm of others. Shamans were believed to have powers to control the spirits and to intercede with them. In times of hardship people turned to them to find out why the spirits were displeased and how matters could be set right. The chief work of shamans lay in diagnosing and curing illness, but through their communication with the spirits they could also predict the weather, indicate where game might be found or put a curse on an enemy or evil-doer. Sometimes they accompanied war-parties to help them to victory.

Many of the myths and legends were considered sacred and could only be recounted by certain people, but others were intended purely for entertainment and could be told by anyone. The time for telling stories was around campfires on long winter evenings, for then the Indians had leisure for such pastimes. Then too, the Indians said, the animals slept and could not be offended by overhearing the many tales which poked fun at them or showed them in a poor light.

Since the arrival of the first European settlers in the sixteenth century, much has changed for the Indians. Little of the traditional way of life remains. Guns have long since ousted bows and arrows, and motorized forms of transport have largely replaced sleds, canoes and horses. Large industrial cities now cover the old hunting grounds. Skin clothing is rarely seen except on special occasions or for the benefit of tourists. While many Indians still farm, hunt and fish in the reservations where they were placed during the nineteenth century, much of their equipment is modern and factory made. Other Indians have gone to seek employment in towns and cities far from their tribal lands.

Many ceremonies have fallen into disuse and many myths are forgotten, for they were not written down, although some were recorded in other ways— on totem poles or in sandpaintings, for example. Yet a great number are still remembered and, around winter firesides, when the animals are asleep, those with long memories continue to instruct their listeners in the customs and values of their forefathers.

A Journey

by Nikki Giovanni

*As you read, imagine you are hearing the
speaker's voice as you start out on your
own journey. What effect does the
speaker's message have on you?*

It's a journey . . . that I propose . . . I am not the
guide . . . nor technical assistant . . . I will be your
fellow passenger . . .

Though the rail has been ridden . . . winter clouds
5 cover . . . autumn's exuberant quilt . . . we must
provide our own guideposts . . .

I have heard . . . from previous visitors . . . the road
washes out sometimes . . . and passengers are
compelled . . . to continue groping . . . or turn back
10 . . . I am not afraid . . .

I am not afraid . . . of rough spots . . . or lonely times
. . . I don't fear . . . the success of this endeavor . . . I
am Ra . . . in a space . . . not to be discovered . . . but
invented . . .

15 I promise you nothing . . . I accept your promise . . .
of the same we are simply riding . . . a wave . . . that
may carry . . . or crash . . .

It's a journey . . . and I want . . . to go . . .

A Mother's Yarn

by James Riordan

*This folk tale is from the Arctic Circle,
where the search for food, warmth, and
wisdom challenges male and female alike.*

Long, long ago, there lived a woman and her
husband with their daughter Nastai.

The old man was a simple soul who did what he
was told. Not that he minded at all, for what he was
not told he did not think of by himself. The mistress,
though, had all her wits about her and there was
little she could not do or did not know.

She was very patient with the old man and would
say, "Come on, old-timer, we need fresh meat." Then
she would take a bow and arrows, and lead the way
into the forest.

Or she would say, "Come along, Grandad, we
need some fish." And she would launch the boat
herself, take up the oars and row out to the middle
of the lake; she would cast the nets and they would
haul in the fish together.

The family lived and prospered, with meat and
fish, fur coats and feather beds. Meanwhile, Nastai
was growing up and learning all her mother knew.
When she was big enough to help, the family lived
even better than before.

But one day, bad times fell upon the old pair—a
sickness swept the land and laid its hand upon them.
In time, the old man survived, but the mistress did
not recover. Before she died, she called Nastai to her.

"I am dying, Daughter. I must leave the old man in

199

your care. See you treat him well." And with that she breathed her last.

Nastai kept her word. She made her father cranberry tea, rubbed bear fat into his skin and gave him venison liver to make him strong. Soon he was fit and well.

Word now went around the camps that the wise woman was dead, leaving the daughter and the old man alone in the cozy house. In time the news reached a distant camp in which there lived a beggarwoman and her daughter. Winds had torn holes in their mud-baked hut, their cooking pots leaked, their fishing nets were rotten, their harpoons broken. But they did not care. They had an old buck deer, and when they wanted food they would hitch him to a sledge and ride from camp to camp to beg for meat. No one would turn them away; such was the custom while folk had food.

When the beggarwoman heard of the old widower, she drove her sledge over plain and hill until she reached the house. How pleased she was to see a herd of reindeer grazing, well-fed dogs running free and the old man sitting outside his cozy home.

"Are you the widower with the herd of deer?" she said.

He nodded.

"Then mind this: I'm now mistress here."

The old man stared.

Nastai had gone for wood and was not at home. When she returned she was surprised to hear strange noises coming from the house. Opening the door, she saw a ragged woman wailing a song with a younger girl. Meanwhile, the old man was banging a spoon upon an empty pot, giggling like an oaf and dribbling down his chin. On the table stood an empty sealskin bag for fire water.

"What's this, Father," Nastai said quietly, "do we have guests?"

"Hold your tongue, girl!" shouted the beggar-woman. "I'm no guest in my own house. I'm mistress here. Is that not so, old man?"

What could he say? His head fell forward in an unwilling nod.

Nastai did as she was told. She brought food at once: cloudberry preserve and fresh-baked rusks. She made up a feather bed and covered it with furs. Meanwhile, the two strangers crammed their mouths with food, before flopping down on the bed to sleep. All the time the old woman wondered how she would rid herself of Nastai.

It was barely light when the beggarwoman awoke. At once she ordered the old man to harness a team of reindeer and load all his fortune on a sled.

"But your good-for-nothing daughter can stay here in her mother's hut," she yelled. "The three of us will live in plenty in my land."

Meekly, the old man harnessed all his reindeer to a sled and began to load it with furs and lace, reindeer hides and feather mattresses, fox and squirrel pelts, axes and harpoons. The two women packed the rest.

Not a crust of bread, not a scrap of meat was left; no fish, no hides, no covers to keep Nastai warm at night. It was cold and dark in the empty hut, and she was hungry. How was she to live? She sat upon the floor and sobbed as if her heart would break.

All of a sudden, she seemed to hear her mother's voice.

"Look about you, Nastai."

She glanced around, searched high and low, but found nothing but a twist of yarn upon the floor. Yes, she remembered now: whenever her mother spun some yarn, she would tear off the thread and drop it on the floor. Nastai now picked it up and once more heard the voice.

"Nastai, remember what I taught you."

She did remember.

Making a loop of yarn out of the thread, she ran to the forest, to a leafy glade where partridges often came to feed on berries. She put her loop on the ground and covered it in leaves. Long and patiently she waited; but at last she snared a lone, lame bird.

She took it home, stripped the veins from the bird's two legs and made another noose.

This time she caught two partridges in her traps. She plucked the feathers from the birds and now had meat for broth. But what could she make it in? She had neither pot, nor fire upon the hearth.

Again a voice was heard.

"Come now, Nastai, remember what I taught you."

Back went the girl into the forest to seek a sturdy silver birch. When she found the right one, she began to tear off strips of bark. These she took home and braided into a bowl, which she coated with clay and left to dry out in the sun. And so she made a bark-clay pot.

Next she scooped up some water into her pot, dropped the partridges in and hung it on two sticks above the hearth. Already she had prepared dry moss, fir cones and twigs for a fire. Now she took two flint stones and struck them together. Thus she worked away until she raised a spark that lit the moss.

Soon the fire blazed; water boiled merrily in the pot and the partridges gave off a delicious smell. Nastai drank the broth and ate the meat, then went to set her traps again.

With each day that passed she caught more birds than ever; she fed on their meat, made traps out of their veins and stored up the feathers and the down. A whole heap of feathers grew up in the corner of the hut and, at night, she slept snug and warm inside. The only trouble was they got into her nose and mouth, making her cough and sneeze.

Then she recalled how her mother had spun some yarn into an eiderdown.

Off she went into the forest again, brought back a strong smooth stick and began to spin a thread from the down and veins; this she wound about the pole, just like a distaff. She spun the yarn and wove herself a cover which she filled with down and feathers. Placing white moss and grass upon the floor, she lay her eiderdown upon it. It was now clean and cozy inside the hut, the hearth fire blazed and meat simmered in the pot. All was well.

As time went by, however, she longed for company. It was then she seemed to hear her mother's voice again.

"Remember, Nastai, what I taught you.'

That gave her an idea.

Off she went to the forest, pulled up a stripling pine and broke off the roots. She braided them with yarn and wove herself a strong lasso. That done, she walked for many days across the plain until she spied a reindeer herd. Hiding in the long white grass, downwind from the herd, she waited patiently. Presently, a little fawn strayed from a doe and wandered towards the clump of grass where Nastai was hiding. All at once, Nastai threw her lasso neatly about the fawn's neck, pulled it towards her and led it home.

She began to tend the fawn, feeding it with moss and grass, and giving it water to drink. The deer soon lost its fear and ran behind her as if she were the mother doe. And she put by some fodder for the fawn, with dry grass and moss, ready for the winter.

Then her thoughts turned to herself, for she had no food to put by, no warm coat, no hat, no boots to wear. Again came her mother's voice.

"Nastai, remember what I taught you."

This time she went down to the lake where there was a willow tree. She snapped off a branch, bent it into a bow and stretched her lasso across both ends. The bow was tough and springy. She then gathered a bundle of smooth sticks, dried them above the hearth and drove sharp flints into the ends.

Winter snow began to fall.

Nastai tethered the fawn close by her hut and went in search of food. She came upon some squirrels hopping along branches, nibbling fir cones; then she spotted a silver fox slinking across the snow, hunting mice. Taking careful aim, she loosed her arrows, killing a squirrel and the fox. She dragged her booty home, where she skinned the two animals, cleaned the furs and hung them to dry.

Next day she went hunting again.

As she returned with more game, she was surprised to see the mother doe standing by her fawn.

So that's that, thought Nastai with sinking heart. She's found her child and will lead it away.

But the doe remained.

That winter much snow fell. It was hard for the two wild deer to clear the snow and eat the moss. So Nastai fed the doe and the little fawn from her supply of moss and grass. Then, to her delight, the buck and his son appeared, followed by other members of the herd.

The girl sat by her warm hearth, sewing a squirrel

coat and foxfur hat with a bird-bone needle, wondering how she was going to keep the herd. When spring came they would surely scatter across the plain. And then once more she harkened to her mother's voice.

"Nastai, remember what I taught you."

Off went Nastai into the forest. She searched long and hard until she found a wolf den with four cubs inside. Fetching the cubs out while the mother was away, she took them home with her.

She fed the cubs on squirrel meat, gave them fresh water to drink, and as they grew she taught them to guard her herd. The cubs obeyed her command, trotted in her steps and were soon as skilled as any dog.

Now she had milk and meat, furs and hides, and plenty of animals for company.

In the meantime, far away, the beggarwoman and her girl were trading away the old man's wealth, while he was hunter, shepherd, cook and cleaner of their house. One year passed, and the fortune was gone. Only the old lame buck remained. So one day, the old woman harnessed it to their rickety sled and got ready to return.

"We're going back to Saami land," she said to him. "You were handy at fishing and hunting there."

She was also thinking to herself: Yes, and that girl will be long dead by now; the wolves will have left no trace.

So all three drove across plain and hill until they reached the Saami land. As they drew near to the old home they were astonished to see a herd of sturdy reindeer grazing, four well-fed dogs standing guard, and there, alongside the well-kept hut, Nastai sitting in her squirrel coat and foxfur hat.

"Welcome home, Father," she said joyfully. "You

must be hungry and tired from your journey. Come inside and try some partridge broth, and rest upon my feather bed."

The old man stared from the herd of reindeer to the old lame buck, from his gentle daughter to the two beggarwomen—and slowly his hand went to his head. Then, for the first time in his life, he opened his mouth and roared like a rutting deer.

"You evil woman, be gone at once. And take your daughter with you!"

With all his strength, he struck the buck upon its rump and off it rushed the way it had come, dragging the two women back to their own land.

And never again did he stray from his daughter's home.

Acknowledgments

Continued from page ii

Peter Bedrick Books: Excerpt from "The First Americans," from *Spirits, Heroes & Hunters from North American Indian Mythology* by Marion Wood. Copyright © 1981 by Eurobook Limited. Reprinted by permission of Peter Bedrick Books, New York.

William Morrow & Company, Inc.: "A Journey," from *Those Who Ride the Night Winds* by Nikki Giovanni. Copyright © 1983 by Nikki Giovanni. By permission of William Morrow & Company, Inc.

Penguin Books USA Inc. and Random House UK Ltd.: "A Mother's Yarn," from *The Woman in the Moon and Other Tales of Forgotten Heroines* by James Riordan. Copyright © 1984 by James Riordan. Used by permission of Dial Books for Young Readers, a division of Penguin Books USA Inc., and by permission of Hutchinson Children's Books, an imprint of Random House UK Ltd.